ANYTHING BUT BALLS

by Willo Ward

in aid of
The Marie Keating Cancer Awareness Fund

Acknowledgments

Jennifer Ward
Ian McKeever, Goodbody McKeever Communications
Viviane Gaine & Killian, Visible Gaine PR
Jo Kramers, Donal O'Sullivan & Niall Maloney,
Murphy's Brewery
Christy Jameson, Future Print Ltd.
Linda, Ciaran, Gerard, Gary & Ronan Keating
Rooney Graphics
Tom Williams, Avenue
Today FM Sports Department, Tim Twomey, Con Murphy,
Stephen Cullinane
Dave Kelly, Michael Mullen
Gerard Kean, John T Murphy Gaisce The President's Award
Liz Murray, Evelyn Sheehan, Barbara Murphy, Sinead
O'Brien, Joeseph Walsh
Louis Walsh, Ian Dempsey, Lorraine Keane, Gemma Doherty,
Pat Gunne
All the girls in the Premiership!!
Andre Varley Photographers, Jason Clarke Photographer
Simona Porta, Veronique Tison
INPHO

Design & Artwork **Rooney Graphics**

Colour Seperations & Printing **Future Print Ltd.**

Paper Merchant **McNaughton Paper Ireland Ltd.**
Printed on Challenger Velvet 100gsm

Book Binding **P&D Finishers**

ISBN 0 9534758 0 8

Copyright Number 003118

Dedication

To Little Liamy, with all my love.

The Marie Keating Cancer Awareness Fund

Hi There

Thank you for you have just helped us to put The Marie Keating Cancer Awareness Mobile Unit on the road.

My name is Linda Keating and together with my brothers Ciaran, Gerard, Gary and Ronan we have set up a fund to raise money for a Cancer Awareness Mobile Unit. We are aiming to raise enough money to put three Units on the road, these Units will travel countrywide and help people become more aware of Cancer and how it can be prevented and even cured, if caught in time, because it is our own ignorance that is killing us and which killed our mother.

We feel as a family that we have lost everything because our Mother was so close to each one of us in a very special way. Mammy was our best friend, thankfully we have each other and we are all very close, but we could still have our Mother with us if she had had a check up sooner or if one of these Units had been made available.

We don't want anybody else going through what we went through, please don't loose your best friend, it could be your Mother, Father, Sister, Brother, Wife, Husband, Girlfriend or Boyfriend. The Unit will carry awareness of all types of Cancer female and male forms.

Thanks to Willo Ward for writing this book, she truly is a wonderful person who has lost her own Mother to Cancer and who is doing this for all of us, thanks Willo, and thank you again for supporting us by buying this book

God bless you all and best wishes.

Ciaran, Gerard, Gary, Ronan and Linda Keating

Introduction

When I first heard that Ronan Keating's mother Marie had died of cancer, my first reaction was of anger. Because I thought to myself "the only reason this is being publicised is because of Ronan being in Boyzone, and what about all the people who die of cancer every day and no one hears a word about it". Then the memories started flooding in, I myself was only 20 years old when my own mother Rosaleen, died of cancer and I suddenly felt a special bond with Ronan even though we had never met, the chance would have been a fine thing!

Then one day as I was flicking through the RTE Guide, I came across an article on Linda Keating, Ronan's sister. That was when I first heard of "The Marie Keating Cancer Awareness Fund".

When I first met Linda, it was as if our two mothers had arranged the whole thing! We connected immediately. We talked for hours about our mothers and why it happened, what could have been done to prevent this. We realised that both our mothers could have been cured of cancer, if it was detected earlier or if we had more knowledge of the disease. We discussed how I could help raise funds for the unit. I had already come up with the concept for "Anything But Balls!", and Linda loved the idea. After she ran it by the family, they agreed to go ahead with it.

Here we go again, sponsors, printers, publicity! I thought there would be no way I was going to be as lucky as last years "Food For Thought". I thought wrong!

Amstel Beer came onboard as the exclusive sponsor, with Christy Jameson of Future Print covering the printing.

Losing a parent at a young age to cancer is sole destroying, you feel like everything in your life is irrelevant, and no one else can even begin to understand how you feel. Cancer can be prevented and even cured. But early detection and fast treatment is so important.

There are so many people all over Ireland who have had the tragedy of watching someone they love fade away. This can be stopped. It has to stop. The Marie Keating Cancer Awareness Fund will fund three Mobile Cancer Units to travel around Ireland. Please use them.

Willo Ward

Murphy Brewery Ireland Limited

Amstel Beer is delighted to be associated with this project. I would like to take this opportunity to thank both Willo Ward and Ian McKeever for the huge amount of time and effort they have put into the completion of this project. Sincerest thanks also to Linda and Ronan Keating and best wishes for the future in their fund raising activities with the Marie Keating Cancer Awareness Fund.

Given Amstel Beer's soccer association with the UEFA Champions League and Irish soccer at League of Ireland and junior league levels this is a very appropriate project for us to undertake. One cannot imagine a more worthwhile cause to support than the valiant efforts being made by the Marie Keating Cancer Awareness Fund to promote cancer awareness and detection in Ireland. For this reason you, the reader, should be proud of the part you have played in contributing towards the fight against cancer in a tangible, meaningful way.

Ms. Jo Kramers
Marketing Director
Murphy Brewery Ireland Limited

Contents

Contents

Contents

Phil Babb

REPUBLIC OF IRELAND

Question 1.
Which football manager do you respect the most and why?
Jack Charlton, because of his great man-management.

Question 2.
How do you feel about the introduction of video evidence and reversible decisions during and after the match?
I think it's a good idea, during a game. Post match decisions shouldn't be allowed though.

Question 3.
What has been your most memorable professional moment and your most embarrassing personal moment?
At this moment in time playing on the '94 World Cup is a great memory and on a personal level I rarely get embarrassed.

Question 4.
If you could change any of the rules in football what would it be?
I would have a referee in each half of the pitch, so they would be able to keep up with play more.

Question 5.

You're playing in the cup final. It's 0 - 0 in the 89th minute. You're tackled by a defender in the penalty box. Would you think about taking a dive to get a penalty?

No! I'd stay on my feet and score!

Question 6.

Do you have an alternative career plan for the day when you retire from professional football?

I'd like to break into the golf industry. I might start arranging charity golf events!

Question 7.

What has been your funniest experience when travelling with your team?

These moments are too X-rated to print!!

Question 8.

Who would you most like to have an Amstel Beer with in the hot tub with you after a big match?

No comment.

Question 9.

What is the most outrageous thing you have ever bought?

I'll keep that one to myself, thank you.

Question 10.

Would you agree with England's Ian Wright that the feeling of scoring a goal is better than sex?

I wouldn't agree with him, maybe he's doing it wrong!

Kevin Ball

SUNDERLAND FOOTBALL CLUB

Question 1.
Which football manager do you respect the most and why?
Alex Ferguson, because when he first went to Man U. people were saying he wouldn't succeed, but he's gone on to be a great manager not only is he good at handling the media, I love the way he sticks up for his players and the look of sheer enjoyment on his face when his team scores a goal.

Question 2.
How do you feel about the introduction of video evidence and reversible decisions during and after the match?
It would interfere with the flow of the game and also may upset fans if certain decision's were altered after they were made.

Question 3.
What has been your most memorable professional moment and your most embarrassing personal moment?
Most memorable moment was lifting the first division championship trophy for Sunderland. Most embarrassing moment was having to run from the pitch to use the toilet and the ref's was the nearest. He wasn't very impressed when he came in and saw me on the throne!

Question 4.
If you could change any of the rules in football what would it be?
After last years play off final it would have to be the penalty decider. It is a cruel way to decide a game!

Question 5.
You're playing in the cup final. It's 0 - 0 all in the 89th minute. You're tackled by a defender in the penalty box. Would you think about taking a dive to get a penalty?
I wouldn't do a blatant one but if I thought in the contest of the tackle I could get a penalty I would probably do it.

Question 6.
Do you have an alternative career plan for the day when you retire from professional football?
Ideally I would like to stay in football. Other than that any other profession would be a new experience for me and I would give it a go.

Question 7.
What has been your funniest experience when travelling with your team?
When we once knew one of our players Martin Gray had removed a kettle from a Hotel, and we said that the Hotel Manager was coming on the bus to search the bags to find the "missing" items, the colour drained from his face.

Question 8.
Who would you most like to have an Amstel Beer with in the hot tub with you after a big match?
Plenty of bubble bath and my wife washing my dirty bits.

Question 9.
What is the most outrageous thing you have ever bought?
I can't say I've bought anything outrageous. I'm fortunate that my wife has an excellent taste in clothes and I always ask her opinion.

Question 10.
Would you agree with England's Ian Wright that the feeling of scoring a goal is better than sex?
As I love both scoring and sex and not always in that order I would have to say they're on a par with each other.

Dave Basset

MANAGER NOTTINGHAM FOREST FOOTBALL CLUB

Question 1.
Which football manager do you respect the most and why?
John Rudger - Port Vale. Shown great loyalty to his club over a long period without being financially rewarded, but at the same time doing an excellent job.

Question 2.
How do you feel about the introduction of video evidence and reversible decisions during and after the match?
Should only be used to justify eitherway between sending off or cautionable decisions.

Question 3.
What has been your most memorable professional moment and your most embarrassing personal moment?
7 promotions. Birth of girls.

Question 4.
If you could change any of the rules in football what would it be?
Injured supposedly having to leave the field when they are perfectly able to continue straight away. Wasting time and penalising the team that has the injured player.

Question 5.
You're playing in the cup final. It's 0 - 0 in the 89th minute. You're tackled by a defender in the penalty box. Would you think about taking a dive to get a penalty?
Not that quick a thinker also likely I would have been substituted by then.

Question 6.
Do you have an alternative career plan for the day when you retire from professional football?
No, just loafing about travelling and doing anything that takes my fancy.

Question 7.
What has been your funniest experience when travelling with your team?
Having trousers and shoes pulled off on train journey back to London by Wimledon players and thrown out window in Hartfordshire. On leaving the train at Ruston had to make way home on tube in socks, underpants, jacket and shirt. Wife utterly amazed when she opened house door.

Question 8.
Who would you most like to have an Amstel Beer with in the hot tub with you after a big match?
Silence is golden.

Question 9.
What is the most outrageous thing you have ever bought?
Photograph book "Sex by Madonna"

Question 10.
Would you agree with England's Ian Wright that the feeling of scoring a goal is better than sex?
No

Dave Beasant

NOTTINGHAM FOREST FOOTBALL CLUB

Question 1.

Which football manager do you respect the most and why?

My current manager, Dave Bassett. He got me started in the pro game and has always been open and honest.

Question 2.

How do you feel about the introduction of video evidence and reversible decisions during and after the match?

It helped me in the case of being sent off in a live game at Reading. The TV replay showed I did not do anything and the decision was reverted.

Question 3.

What has been your most memorable professional moment and your most embarrassing personal moment?

Winning the FA Cup with Wimbledon and playing for England. A match for Chelsea -v- Norwich in which I let a couple of bad goals in.

Question 4.

If you could change any of the rules in football what would it be?

No Comment.

Question 5.
You're playing in the cup final. It's 0 - 0 in the 89th minute. You're tackled by a defender in the penalty box. Would you think about taking a dive to get a penalty?
I'd love to take a dive, being a goalkeeper of course!

Question 6.
Do you have an alternative career plan for the day when you retire from professional football?
Hopefully I'll stay in the game in a coaching job, probably working with keepers.

Question 7.
What has been your funniest experience when travelling with your team?
There's many, but one, at Wimbledon our physio Derek French could not swim, and we had a boat trip where Derek was dangled over the side held only by his ankles. He wasn't amused!!!

Question 8.
Who would you most like to have an Amstel Beer with in the hot tub with you after a big match?
My two boys currently 10 & 12. At the end of a Premier match, all three of us having just played!

Question 9.
What is the most outrageous thing you have ever bought?
My classic Aston Martin V8 Volante!

Question 10.
Would you agree with England's Ian Wright that the feeling of scoring a goal is better than sex?
Having never scored I wouldn't know, but I don't think I could go along with Wrighty!

Mark Beeney

LEEDS UNITED FOOTBALL CLUB

Question 1.
Which football manager do you respect the most and why?
John Steel - Manager Maidstone 87/88. Because he gave me my first break in football.

Question 2.
How do you feel about the introduction of video evidence and reversible decisions during and after the match?
Yes why not, if it works in Rugby why not football.

Question 3.
What has been your most memorable professional moment and your most embarrassing personal moment?
Winning the league with Maidstone (GM Conference). Played against Guisborough - went out to catch a ball and it sailed over my head into the back of the net!

Question 4.
If you could change any of the rules in football what would it be?
Offside rule. Put a line 35 yards out from the goal line and only have offsides goal sides of the line.

Question 5.

You're playing in the cup final. It's 0-0 in the 89th minute. You're tackled by a defender in the penalty box. Would you think about taking a dive to get a penalty?

Yes, definitely.

Question 6.

Do you have an alternative career plan for the day when you retire from professional football?

Not really as yet. But I could be a bootleg booze importer! It's very cheap in France!

Question 7.

What has been your funniest experience when travelling with your team?

Watching Robert Molenaar's face as the plane we were travelling on went into crash land! - Really memorable.

Question 8.

Who would you most like to have an Amstel Beer with in the hot tub with you after a big match?

Demi Moore and Cathy Lloyd, Caprice and anyone who is willing!

Question 9.

What is the most outrageous thing you have ever bought?

Porche 991 Convertible.

Question 10.

Would you agree with England's Ian Wright that the feeling of scoring a goal is better than sex?

No, but I have only scored once, with the youth team!

George Best

EX MANCHESTER UNITED AND NORTHERN IRELAND

Question 1.
Which football manager do you respect the most and why?
Sir Matt Busby, because after loosing half a great side in 1958, 10 years later he won the European Cup. He played football with a laugh and a love.

Questrion 2.
How do you feel about the introduction of video evidence and reversible decisions during and after the match?
During the game as in other sports, try it! Afterwards it's too late.

Question 3.
What has been your most memorable professional moment and your most embarrassing personal moment?
1966 verses Benfica in Lisbon 5 - 1. Northampton 1971, 6 goals in the cup. When marrying my wife, Alex picking up my wedding ring and putting it on her finger.

Question 4.
If you could change any of the rules in football what would it be?
Bring back tackling. To make it a mans game again.

Question 5.
You're playing in the cup final. It's 0 - 0 in the 89th minute. You're tackled by a defender in the penalty box. Would you think about taking a dive to get a penalty?
I'd beat the tackle and score!

Question 6.
Did you have an alternative career plan for the day when you retired from professional football?
There is no alternative after football.

Question 7.
What has been your funniest experience when travelling with your team?
After the Benfica game in 1966, I was chased by a Benfica fan with a knife, I thought he wanted to kill me. But all he wanted was a lock of my hair!

Question 8.
Who would you most like to have an Amstel Beer with in the hot tub with you after a big match?
The player who scored the winning goal in the European Cup Final.

Question 9.
What is the most outrageous thing you have ever bought?
A white Rolls Royce, when living in digs at 21!

Question 10.
Would you agree with England's Ian Wright that the feeling of scoring a goal is better than sex?
Yes & No!

Leon Braithwaite

ST. PATRICK'S FOOTBALL CLUB

Question 1.
Which football manager do you respect the most and why?
Fabio Capello the former AC Milan Boss. He managed one of the most successful sides of the late 80's early 90's there has ever been in European soccer. He managed to get players playing to their full capacity and got respected by some of footballs greats as Rudd Gullit, Marco Van Basten and Franco Baresi.

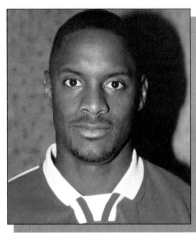

Question 2.
How do you feel about the introduction of video evidence and reversible decisions during and after the match?
I strongly disagree with this, as this will slow down the game and make it something of which cricketers are used to, boring! Mistakes will always happen and bad decisions etc. which adds to the reality of the game, why make it Americanised.

Question 3.
What has been your most memorable professional moment and your most embarrassing personal moment?
My most memorable moment must be scoring my first league goal at Fulham's Craven Cottage. My most embarrassing must be against Bolton, I had taken on two players and was about to cross the ball when I miskicked the ball and fell on my face.

Question 4.
If you could change any of the rules in football what would it be?
The tackle from behind. If you win the ball it should be allowed, but then if you don't then rightly so, and be punished.

Question 5.
You're playing in the cup final. It's 0-0 in the 89th minute. You're tackled by a defender in the penalty box. Would you think about taking a dive to get a penalty?
If it was for my country to qualify for the World Cup then yes I would. Otherwise no way!

Question 6.
Do you have an alternative career plan for the day when you retire from professional football?
To become a music producer, which was what I studied for, or coach kids football.

Question 7.
What has been your funniest experience when travelling with your team?
No comment.

Question 8.
Who would you most like to have an Amstel Beer with in the hot tub with you after a big match?
My love of my life, Sandra Mertens, if not then the actress Jennifer Lopez.

Question 9.
What is the most outrageous thing you have ever bought?
Green hair dye!

Question 10.
Would you agree with England's Ian Wright that the feeling of scoring a goal is better than sex?
Yes!

Michael Branch

EVERTON FOOTBALL CLUB

Question 1.
Which football manager do you respect the most and why?
Alex Ferguson, for his achievements.

Question 2.
How do you feel about the introduction of video evidence and reversible decisions during and after the match?
I don't think it will be a good idea.

Question 3.
What has been your most memorable professional moment and your most embarrassing personal moment?
Making my debut at Old Trafford.

Question 4.
If you could change any of the rules in football what would it be?
Offside rule.

Question 5.
You're playing in the cup final. It's 0-0 in the 89th minute. You're tackled by a defender in the penalty box. Would you think about taking a dive to get a penalty?
Yes.

Question 6.
**Do you have an alternative career plan for the
day when you retire from professional football?**
Coaching in America.

Question 7.
**What has been your funniest experience when travelling with
your team?**
None yet!

Question 8.
**Who would you most like to have an Amstel Beer with in the
hot tub with you after a big match?**
Cameron Diaz (film star).

Question 9.
What is the most outrageous thing you have ever bought?
Tank top!

Question 10.
**Would you agree with England's Ian Wright that the feeling of
scoring a goal is better than sex?**
Yes.

Shay Brennan

EX MANCHESTER UNITED AND REPUBLIC OF IRELAND

Question 1.
Which football manager do you respect the most and why?
Sir Matt Busby because he built a winning European Cup side, out of the disaster of the Munich air crash.

Question 2.
How do you feel about the introduction of video evidence and reversible decisions during and after the match?
Do not agree. .

Question 3.
What has been your most memorable professional moment and your most embarrassing personal moment?
Playing for Manchester United against Sheffield Wednesday - 1st match after Munich air disater and scoring 2 goals. D. G. against Benfica - European Cup quarter final.

Question 4.
If you could change any of the rules in football what would it be?
Take out penalties in extra time and play for golden goals only.

Question 5.
You're playing in the cup final. It's 0 -0 all in the 89th minute. You're tackled by a defender in the penalty box. Would you think about taking a dive to get a penalty?
Yes!!!

Question 6.
Did you have an alternative career plan for the day when you retired from professional football?
Retired 1972. Would like to have lived on my earnings, however I am a gambler and like a drink, so I have "Her Indoors" working.

Question 7.
What has been your funniest experience when travelling with your team?
Travelling with Nobby Stiles, always good for a laugh. Walking into glass doors, tie always in soup bowls, going to loo at functions, ending up sitting at wrong function on return from loo!!

Question 8.
Who would you most like to have an Amstel Beer with in the hot tub with you after a big match?
Ronnie Barker, late Peter Sellars and Nobby Stiles.

Question 9.
What is the most outrageous thing you have ever bought?
Very large stuffed Mynah bird from Australia, took up an aircraft seat. It was a gift for my six year old daughter. She was terrified of it!!!!!

Question 10.
Would you agree with England's Ian Wright that the feeling of scoring a goal is better than sex?
Can't answer, my wife is sitting beside me!!!!

Ian Brightwell

COVENTRY CITY FOOTBALL CLUB

Question 1.
Which football manager do you respect the most and why?
I've worked under 14 managers during my years with Manchester City and Coventry and I've respected them all in different ways. Every one had their individual strengths and weaknesses.

Question 2.
How do you feel about the introduction of video evidence and reversible decisions during and after the match?
I think it would be good for split decisions i.e. has the ball crossed the line or not and off the ball situations i.e. punches, headbuts etc.

Question 3.
What has been your most memorable professional moment and your most embarrassing personal moment?
Most memorable was my 1st team debut at Manchester City -v- Wimbledon in 1986. Worst moment is scoring an own goal.

Question 4.
If you could change any of the rules in football what would it be?
Keep it as it is.

Question 5.
You're playing in the cup final. It's 0 - 0 in the 89th minute.

You're tackled by a defender in the penalty box. Would you think about taking a dive to get a penalty?
No, because a) you can be booked and b) people would lose respect professionally c) if it is a foul you will fall over anyway!

Question 6.
Do you have an alternative career plan for the day when you retire from professional football?
I have several properties and a company that rent those properties. I would like to stay in football i.e. coaching.

Question 7.
What has been your funniest experience when travelling with your team?
It's hard to think of one particular incident without incriminating people. But maybe when one unattached member of the team thought he'd pulled a really attractive girl, unfortunately for him he found out it was a man!

Question 8.
Who would you most like to have an Amstel Beer with in the hot tub with you after a big match?
My girlfriend Helen, only she doesn't drink beer so it would have to be Ale MacPherson.

Question 9.
What is the most outrageous thing you have ever bought?
A nasty yellow leather jacket about 10 years ago.

Question 10.
Would you agree with England's Ian Wright that the feeling of scoring a goal is better than sex?
I'd like to say I scored more goals than I have sex. Unfortunately I'm not in the opponents box that often so I can't agree with Wrightys comment.

Tommy Byrne

BOHEMIAN FOOTBALL CLUB

Question 1.
Which football manager do you respect the most and why?
Arsene Wenger. He stuck to his guns and changed the way Arsenal prepare and play.

Question 2.
How do you feel about the introduction of video evidence and reversible decisions during and after the match?
Good providing you have nothing to hide.

Question 3.
What has been your most memorable professional moment and your most embarrassing personal moment?
No comment.

Question 4.
If you could change any of the rules in football what would it be?
Two refs, because one ref. in the league of Ireland is not enough.

Question 5.
You're playing in the cup final. It's 0 -0 all in the 89th minute. You're tackled by a defender in the penalty box. Would you think about taking a dive to get a penalty?
No.

Question 6.
Do you have an alternative career plan for the day when you retire from professional football?
Yes, coaching.

Question 7.
What has been your funniest experience when travelling with your team?
Alan Byrne losing his passport in Romania.

Question 8.
Who would you most like to have an Amstel Beer with in the hot tub with you after a big match?
Melinda Messinger.

Question 9.
What is the most outrageous thing you have ever bought?
Food for Eoin Mullen!

Question 10.
Would you agree with England's Ian Wright that the feeling of scoring a goal is better than sex?
Who is he sleeping with?

Danni Cadamarteri

EVERTON FOOTBALL CLUB

Question 1.
Which football manager do you respect the most and why?
Alex Ferguson, for his achievements at Manchester United.

Question 2.
How do you feel about the introduction of video evidence and reversible decisions during and after the match?
It's a good idea.

Question 3.
What has been your most memorable professional moment and your most embarrassing personal moment?
Scoring in the Merseyside derby.

Question 4.
If you could change any of the rules in football what would it be?
The back pass rule.

Question 5.
You're playing in the cup final. It's 0-0 in the 89th minute. You're tackled by a defender in the penalty box. Would you think about taking a dive to get a penalty?
Yes

Question 6.
Do you have an alternative career plan for the day when you retire from professional football?
Drama.

Question 7.
What has been your funniest experience when travelling with your team?
None yet!

Question 8.
Who would you most like to have an Amstel Beer with in the hot tub with you after a big match?
Ian Wright

Question 9.
What is the most outrageous thing you have ever bought?
Many shoes.

Question 10.
Would you agree with England's Ian Wright that the feeling of scoring a goal is better than sex?
Yes!

Steve Chettle

NOTTINGHAM FOREST FOOTBALL CLUB

Question 1.
Which football manager do you respect the most and why?
Brian Clough because he introduced me into football and I also won most of my honours under his management.

Question 2.
How do you feel about the introduction of video evidence and reversible decisions during and after the match?
I don't think there is any need for video evidence in the game because you will lose the spontaneity in the game, plus there will be nothing to argue about down the pub!

Question 3.
What has been your most memorable professional moment and your most embarrassing personal moment?
Captaining England U 21's and winning the League Cup twice is my most memorable moment. Being taken by surprise on the golf course and having to clean myself up with my underwear.

Question 4.
If you could change any of the rules in football what would it be?
I would change the rule to stop anyone changing any other rules in the lovely game of football.

Question 5.
You're playing in the cup final. It's 0-0 all in the 89th minute. You're tackled by a defender in the penalty box. Would you think about taking a dive to get a penalty?
Of course.

Question 6.
Do you have an alternative career plan for the day when you retire from professional football?
Not at this moment in time.

Question 7.
What has been your funniest experience when travelling with your team?
Being arrested on the way to Sheffield for speeding on the hard shoulder in the team bus.

Question 8.
Who would you most like to have an Amstel Beer with in the hot tub with you after a big match?
Kylie Minogue holding another large bottle of Amstel.

Question 9.
What is the most outrageous thing you have ever bought?
A bright PINK pair of shoes which I wore only on a handful of occasions.

Question 10.
Would you agree with England's Ian Wright that the feeling of scoring a goal is better than sex?
I score about once a season, so I'd have to say sex is a lot more often and enjoyable.

Jeff Clarke

ST. PATRICK'S FOOTBALL CLUB

Question 1.
Which football manager do you respect the most and why?
Alex Ferguson, because of all the controversy which he is surrounded by never affects his way of approaching things. Being rated Britain's most hated person has never changed his way of managing. His policy of giving youths a chance has always been my No 1. for respect.

Question 2.
How do you feel about the introduction of video evidence and reversible decisions during and after the match?
I think they should leave things the same way they have been for the last 60 years. If they introduce videos for goals then football in general will be the one to pay for it. Referees make bad calls both ways so if you are on the side where there was a goal counted against you that just means you'll have to go and score two!

Question 3.
What has been your most memorable professional moment and your most embarrassing personal moment?
My most memorable moment was when my U-20's national team won the U-21's World Cup qualifying tournament in Mexico '96.

Question 4.
If you could change any of the rules in football what would it be?
You should be able to tackle from behind and win the ball. The current law states if you tackle from behind you get cautioned.

Question 5.

You're playing in the cup final. It's 0-0 all in the 89th minute. You're tackled by a defender in the penalty box. Would you think about taking a dive to get a penalty?

I would think about it, yes. It depends on who I am playing against and how much the match really meant to me. Being Canadian means if I am playing against the USA then you can count on me falling!

Question 6.

Do you have an alternative career plan for the day when you retire from professional football?

Complete my university degree in both crimanology and psychology and also take enough coaching courses to be regarded as a well documented and travelled manager.

Question 7.

What has been your funniest experience when travelling with your team?

We were travelling back from a match going 90 mph. approx. and the guy in the front seat threw a pizza box out the window, hitting the windshield of the car trailing us and causing a slight car accident!

Question 8.

Who would you most like to have an Amstel Beer with in the hot tub with you after a big match?

Vanessa Williams. Now I have a question for you. Are our clothes on or off?

Question 9.

What is the most outrageous thing you have ever bought?

A prostitute for one of my buddies stag night! It was the most awkward thing being a John but it was worth the laugh.

Question 10.

Would you agree with England's Ian Wright that the feeling of scoring a goal is better than sex?

Depends who the sex is with!

David Connolly

REPUBLIC OF IRELAND

Question 1.
Which football manager do you respect the most and why?
I respect any manager who treats his players well, Supports them in public and is a good manager. Alex Ferguson seems to fit these criteria.

Question 2.
How do you feel about the introduction of video evidence and reversible decisions during and after the match?
I feel referees make too many mistakes and nowadays these mistakes are too costly to be overlooked. So I do feel something needs to be done, but as to exactly what I don't know. Maybe a "3rd eye" as in cricket, but how you would introduce this to football without losing the flow of the game is to be seen.

Question 3.
What has been your most memorable professional moment and your most embarrassing personal moment?
Scoring 3 for Watford on my 1st full game. Also making my debut and scoring my 1st goal for Ireland are the highlights for me. Scoring 3 for Ireland was a high as well. When I played for Watford -v- Wolves, I came on as a sub and five minutes later I had to come off after making an absolute idiot of myself.

Question 4.
If you could change any of the rules in football what would it be?
I would leave football pretty much as it is.

Question 5.
You're playing in the cup final. It's 0 - 0 in the 89th minute. You're tackled by a defender in the penalty box. Would you think about taking a dive to get a penalty?
Yes!

Question 6.
Do you have an alternative career plan for the day when you retire from professional football?
No! I'm too young to think about what to do when I'm finished.

Question 7.
What has been your funniest experience when travelling with your team?
I've had loads with Ireland, most of which are concerning Mark Kennedy. He is mad and is a great lad to have around. I wouldn't disclose some of the funniest stories because they'd have to be censored!

Question 8.
Who would you most like to have an Amstel Beer with in the hot tub with you after a big match?
Andrea from the Corrs.Melanie Sykes, Kate Moss, Helena Christianson. Any of the above, I'm not fussy!

Question 9.
What is the most outrageous thing you have ever bought?
An expensive watch.

Question 10.
Would you agree with England's Ian Wright that the feeling of scoring a goal is better than sex?
No comment!

Terry Conroy

EX REPUBLIC OF IRELAND

Question 1.
Which football manager do you respect the most and why?
Alex Ferguson, he has improved every club he ever managed. From East Fife, to Manchester United. He has kept Man Utd. at the very top for the past six seasons, and has the rare ability to keep his star players happy. You rarely hear any noises of discontent coming from within Old Trafford.

Question 2.
How do you feel about the introduction of video evidence and reversible decisions during and after the match?
I feel that the introduction of video help will be good for the game, but only issues such as determining penalty kicks and whether the ball has crossed the line. Referee's still have to be in charge and that responsibility should not be diminished

Questiuon 3.
What has been your most memorable professional moment and your most embarrassing personal moment?
The ambition of most kids growing up is to be a professional footballer. Also he can imagine himself playing at Wembley. I have played in a League Cup Final at Wembley, when beating Chelsea 2 -1. I scored the first goal and made the second much to the delight of the

large contingent from Cabra. Also playing for Ireland at Wembley. Receiving a cut on my head. The trainer, at the time, had to bandage my head and send me back on. The colour of the bandage was PINK! Can you imagine that, particularly when the game was televised!

Question 4.
If you could change any of the rules in football what would it be?
Scrap the offside law.

Question 5.
You're playing in the cup final. It's 0 - 0 in the 89th minute. You're tackled by a defender in the penalty box. Would you think about taking a dive to get a penalty?
Most definitely No. In my playing days only Francis Lee was considered a diver. Nowadays I suppose it's quite normal to do it.

Question 6.
Did you have an alternative career plan for the day when you retire from professional football?
I have been retired since 1981. I am still looking for a career that will fulfil my life but if I live to be 100, I know I will still be searching. It's the greatest job in the world bar none, getting well paid for something you love doing. Shangri La, Utopia, call it what you will!

Question 7.
What has been your funniest experience when travelling with your team?
On one occasion, I was present when a former President of the FAI called a press conference because he was fed up with the criticism heaped on him by the press. His famous words were "Certain people have been making allegations about me, and I won't rest until I find out who those "Alligators" are?" Follow that.

Question 8.
Who would you most like to have an Amstel Beer with in the hot tub with you after a big match?
Another one, just to keep it company!

Question 9.
What is the most outrageous thing you have ever bought?
A pair of platform shoes, with 12 inch heels. I thought they were the business, but nobody else did. Tony Waddington my manager at Stoke told me in no uncertain terms to get rid. Otherwise the club could not risk insuring me against breaking my neck!

Question 10.
Would you agree with England's Ian Wright that the feeling of scoring a goal is better than sex?
It depends on the goal. If I scored a tap in from 2 yards I wouldn't get that excited. However I have been known to score great goals, and maybe then I would consider it to be on a par. Whatever way you look at it, it's still scoring isn't it.

Ken Cunningham

REPUBLIC OF IRELAND

Question 1.
Which football manager do you respect the most and why?
Mick McCarthy, for giving me my first major wage increase up becoming manager at Millwall, what a gentleman!

Question 2.
How do you feel about the introduction of video evidence and reversible decisions during and after the match?
I would not favour anything which would disrupt or interfere with the fast-flowing nature of the game.

Question 3.
What has been your most memorable professional moment and your most embarrassing personal moment?
Captaining my country against the Czech Republic this year and tripping over the advertising boards placed in the centre circle during the warm up in a game against Tranmere at Prenton Park, many moons ago. I would like to think my vision has improved a lot since!!!

Question 4.
If you could change any of the rules in football what would it be?
Introduce a transfer window at one or two stages of the season as is used in a number of European Leagues.

Question 5.
You're playing in the cup final. It's 0 - 0 in the 89th minute.

You're tackled by a defender in the penalty box. Would you think about taking a dive to get a penalty?

Having travelled so far into the oppositions penalty area the likelihood is that a severe noise bleed would hinder my progress before resisting any challenges!!!!

Question 6.
Do you have an alternative career plan for the day when you retire from professional football?

As a professional golfer, if and when I can straighten up my dog-hook off the tee and bad case of the yipes on the greens!

Question 7.
What has been your funniest experience when travelling with your team?

Seeing our chairman Sam Hamman's new sheepskin jacket disappearing out of the emergency hatch of our coach, followed by loud cheers as it disappeared under the wheels of a juggernaut following behind. The perpetrators have never been brought to justice!!!!

Question 8.
Who would you most like to have an Amstel Beer with in the hot tub with you after a big match?

Mark Kinsella, it usually takes that amount to get him bladdered!!!!

Question 9.
What is the most outrageous thing you have ever bought?

Sad to say probably a hand painted Bodhran which I purchased in Clifton, Connamara some time. It takes pride of place in my flat in London, although I fear that my neighbours are not amongst my greatest fans!!!!

Question 10.
Would you agree with England's Ian Wright that the feeling of scoring a goal is better than sex?

Seeing as thought it is 5 years since I last scored a goal, when coincidentally is roughly the last time I had sex!!!! I must decline to answer on the grounds of amnesia!!!!!!

Rory Delap

REPUBLIC OF IRELAND

Question 1.
Which football manager do you respect the most and why?
Alex Ferguson, because he got so much stick in his 1st couple of seasons.

Question 2.
How do you feel about the introduction of video evidence and reversible decisions during and after the match?
As long as it's for important decisions only.

Question 3.
What has been your most memorable professional moment and your most embarrassing personal moment?
Winning the Auto-Windscreen Shield with Carlisle, winning my 1st U21 cap & 1st full cap. Being sick on the pitch at Pride Park in front of 30,000 people.

Question 4.
If you could change any of the rules in football what would it be?
When injured players have to leave the pitch when they can carry on as soon as they walk off.

Question 5.
You're playing in the cup final. It's 0 -0 all in the 89th minute. You're tackled by a defender in the penalty box. Would you think about taking a dive to get a penalty?
Probably. Yes!

Question 6.
Do you have an alternative career plan for the day when you retire from professional football?
Yes, hopefully I will be able to open a pub, restaurant or hotel.

Question 7.
What has been your funniest experience when travelling with your team?
At Carlisle David Reeves had a false rubber hand and a waitress nearly had a heart attack when he pulled his arm away and left the hand on the table, but you probably had to be there.

Question 8.
Who would you most like to have an Amstel Beer with in the hot tub with you after a big match?
Melanie Sykes.

Question 9.
What is the most outrageous thing you have ever bought?
A pair of biker boots!

Question 10.
Would you agree with England's Ian Wright that the feeling of scoring a goal is better than sex?
No!

Jason Dodd

SOUTHAMPTON FOOTBALL CLUB

Question 1.
Which football manager do you respect the most and why?
Ex-Southampton boss - Chris Nicholl. He gave me my big break from non-league football and started my career off. Also he commanded respect of all his players some who were International players.

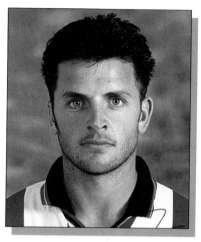

Question 2.
How do you feel about the introduction of video evidence and reversible decisions during and after the match?
If it was to improve close decisions and give the officials more help then it could improve the tough decisions they make and limit some of the mistakes they make.

Question 3.
What has been your most memorable professional moment and your most embarrassing personal moment?
My home debut for Saints against Liverpool. We won 4 - 1 and I still remember well. One of my team mates was a substitute and as he tore his jumper off he had no shirt on! He'd forgot to put it on and had to get someone to run to the changing rooms and get it.

Question 4.
If you could change any of the rules in football what would it be?
"Bookings" given out so cheaply for minor offences.

Question 5.
You're playing in the cup final. It's 0-0 in the 89th minute. You're tackled by a defender in the penalty box. Would you think about taking a dive to get a penalty?
No. Cheating by diving is trying to con to win a football match.

Question 6.
Do you have an alternative career plan for the day when you retire from professional football?
Most players try to put the thoughts of life after football at the back of their mind.

Question 7.
What has been your funniest experience when travelling with your team?
Being late for a match and having to get changed on the bus. People were giving you some funny looks from outside.

Question 8.
Who would you most like to have an Amstel Beer with in the hot tub with you after a big match?
My wife and baby girl.

Question 9.
What is the most outrageous thing you have ever bought?
Some of the boys would probably say some of the "GEAR" I buy. Jealous or what!

Question 10.
Would you agree with England's Ian Wright that the feeling of scoring a goal is better than sex?
I don't remember the feelings of scoring a goal that often, but he has. So he knows more about it than me.

Richard Dryden

SOUTHAMPTON FOOTBALL CLUB

Question 1.

Which football manager do you respect the most and why?

Terry Cooper- my manager at Exeter and Birmingham. He made ordinary players into good players.

Question 2.

How do you feel about the introduction of video evidence and reversible decisions during and after the match?

It would slow the pace of the game too much. After the match it could reverse decisions such as dodgy sendings off.

Question 3.

What has been your most memorable professional moment and your most embarrassing personal moment?

Starting my first premiership game for Southampton against Chelsea live on Sky! Scoring the own goal on the last game of that season that almost relegated us!

Question 4.

If you could change any of the rules in football what would it be?

Automatic bookings for diving.

Question 5.
You're playing in the cup final. It's 0 - 0 in the 89th minute. You're tackled by a defender in the penalty box. Would you think about taking a dive to get a penalty?
No definitely not! (See answer to Question 4)

Question 6.
Do you have an alternative career plan for the day when you retire from professional football?
Not at the moment.

Question 7.
What has been your funniest experience when travelling with your team?
When I was at Bristol City, we were half way to Brighton when another player noticed I had two different trainers on!

Question 8.
Who would you most like to have an Amstel Beer with in the hot tub with you after a big match?
My wife, Lindsay.

Question 9.
What is the most outrageous thing you have ever bought?
A couple of my holiday shirts!

Question 10.
Would you agree with England's Ian Wright that the feeling of scoring a goal is better than sex?
I haven't scored many goals!

Damien Duff

REPUBLIC OF IRELAND

Question 1.
Which football manager do you respect the most and why?
Roy Hodgson, for giving me a chance and has thought me so much

Question 2.
How do you feel about the introduction of video evidence and reversible decisions during and after the match?
Does not interest me. No thoughts on it.

Question 3.
What has been your most memorable professional moment and your most embarrassing personal moment?
International debut, my first goal for Blackburn. None as yet, thankfully.

Question 4.
If you could change any of the rules in football what would it be?
Happy the way it is.

Question 5.
You're playing in the cup final. It's 0 -0 all in the 89th minute. You're tackled by a defender in the penalty box. Would you think about taking a dive to get a penalty?
Yes! No doubt about it.

Question 6.
Do you have an alternative career plan for the day when you retire from professional football?
More football!

Question 7.
What has been your funniest experience when travelling with your team?
None that stands out in my mind.

Question 8.
Who would you most like to have an Amstel Beer with in the hot tub with you after a big match?
The Corrs (Girls).

Question 9.
What is the most outrageous thing you have ever bought?
No comment.

Question 10.
Would you agree with England's Ian Wright that the feeling of scoring a goal is better than sex?
Yes!

Eamon Dunphy

Question 1.
Which football manager do you respect the most and why?
Arsene Wenger, because of his achievements with Arsenal. He's very intelligent. He had made good players better which is the essence of good management. An outstanding manager.

Question 2.
How do you feel about the introduction of video evidence and reversible decisions during and after the match?
I think it should be used in exceptional cases, but not as an every match occurrence. It is a difficult area because you don't want to upset the essential elements of the sport, but if it can help right injustices then it should be used.

Question 3.
What has been your most memorable professional moment and your most embarrassing personal moment?
I played in 3 promotion winning sides, and I think for a lesser player getting promotion is the equivalent of winning the Championship. I was with Millwall, Charlton and Reading and they were the most memorable moments for me. I was one of the leaders in the campaign to get an Irish Manager who was allowed pick the team and when we

achieved this democracy with Mick Meagan's appointment we played Austria at Dalymount. I asked Mick to substitute me at half-time because I was exhausted by the campaign and frankly I was an embarrassment to democracy!

Question 4.
If you could change any of the rules in football what would it be?
I'd like to see the offside rule amended so that you could only be offside in an area 25 yards from goal. I think the game favours defenders too much and I'd like to see a liberalisation of that.

Question 5.
You're playing in the cup final. It's 0 -0 all in the 89th minute. You're tackled by a defender in the penalty box. Would you think about taking a dive to get a penalty?
Not consciously no.

Question 6.
Did you retire have an alternative career plan for the day when you retire from professional football?
Roughly yes, to go into journalism, to write books about the game. I prepared myself while still playing, I wrote a book as a player and I had a natural aptitude for it and a desire to talk about the game. I worked very hard at the print journalism. All other media work, I fell into by accident. I didn't plan them but was lucky enough to do them.

Question 7.
What has been your funniest experience when travelling with your team?
A lot of funny experiences, I was one of the lads at the back of the bus. There was an incident at Millwall, when we led Gordon Hill to believe he was going to be made famous and interviewed. It went on for about 2 weeks and culminated in us throwing a bucket of water

over Gordon in front of a bogus photographer with a camera with no film in it.

Question 8.
Who would you most like to have an Amstel Beer with in the hot tub with you after a big match?
Meryl Streep or perhaps her daughter!

Question 9.
What is the most outrageous thing you have ever bought?
A video camera, when they first came out for vast amounts of money, which I never used.

Question 10.
Would you agree with England's Ian Wright that the feeling of scoring a goal is better than sex?
No, definitely not.

Alan Evans

EX-ASTON VILLA AND SCOTLAND

Question 1.
Which football manager do you respect the most and why?
Good question! Arsene Wenger, since he's come to this country, has organised the place and got them winning things, which is the main point. From what you hear about the camp the players enjoy the type of working that he gives them, educating them on the food aspect and the fitness aspect. He's done a very good job at Arsenal.

ASTON VILLA F.C.

PREPARED

Question 2.
How do you feel about the introduction of video evidence and reversible decisions during and after the match?
I think it's inevitable that it's going to come in, it's virtually impossible for the referee to get everything right and I think if they can be assisted in some way then that's got to happen. On the point of red cards and yellow cards, again I think that its showing the referees have made mistakes on a regular basis and admit to making mistakes then players shouldn't be suspended when they haven't committed the suggested fowl.

Question 3.
What has been your most memorable professional moment and your most embarrassing personal moment?
My Villa days when we won the European Cup, 1982. Playing for

Scotland in the world cup in Spain in the same year. Whenever I have been sent off. It happened about four times in my career, when you have actually done something completely stupid, and you have to have a long walk from the pitch to the dressing room and everyone is looking at you. When I got sent off against Coventry City for head butting Tommy Hutchenson, my mother and father had come down from Scotland to watch me play and I only lasted about 20 mins in the game! I did deserve to be sent off.

Question 4.
If you could change any of the rules in football what would it be?
The problem nowadays, talking as a defender, I think they have taken away a lot, tackles from behind. I think if the ball is won and players can get their feet around the ball and win it back, I don't think there is anything wrong with that. I think they have gone too far, by taking that away from defenders. Also the back pass rule, as a defender, if you can slide into a challenge and manage to knock the ball back to your keeper that is an art, it's an ability in itself, again they have taken that away from defenders. I am probably being a little bit selfish thinking only as a defender.

Question 5.
You're playing in the cup final. It's 0-0 in the 89th minute. You're tackled by a defender in the penalty box. Would you think about taking a dive to get a penalty?
No, I don't think you can think about diving, If there's contact made in the box and you feel your going to loose your balance then you go over, you don't stop yourself from going over. But I would never ever dive.

Question 6.
Did you have an alternative career plan for the day when you retired from professional football?
I had an alternative when I was a youngster, if I had stayed in school instead of leaving to play football, I would have liked to have been a Doctor. But after the game I wanted to stay in the coaching, management side.

Question 7.
What has been your funniest experience when travelling with your team?
One of the funniest / strangest was when we travelled with Aston Villa to Russia. We were way out in no mans land, we were staying in a small hotel our of the way, it was winter, the hotel wasn't really set up for looking after professional footballers. The whole 3/4 days there, we had to bring our own food, when we first arrived it was very late in the evening and there was no time really to get our own food and they gave us some soup and bread. I remember seeing some dead insects in the bread! It was funny at the time, we had a good laugh.

Question 8.
Who would you most like to have an Amstel Beer with in the hot tub with you after a big match?
Oh, I couldn't answer that one!

Question 9.
What is the most outrageous thing you have ever bought?
I think when you go on trips particularly to Europe, you seem to feel like you have to buy something when you're in a foreign country, when we were in Iceland mohair jackets were very popular out there because of the weather. I remember buying two, one for myself and one for my wife at quite a cost. We never ever wore them.

Question 10.
Would you agree with England's Ian Wright that the feeling of scoring a goal is better than sex?
I've scored quite a few goals. It's a thrill you get quite a good buzz from it, I wouldn't say better than, but it depends on the individual I suppose.

Les Ferdinand

TOTTENHAM HOTSPUR FOOTBALL CLUB

Question 1.
Which football manager do you respect the most and why?
Kevin Keegan and Gerry Francis. For the way in which they asked their players to go out and play football as well as the way in which they motivate their players and communicated with them.

Question 2.
How do you feel about the introduction of video evidence and reversible decisions during and after the match?
Video evidence will become a major thing in football because football is so big nowadays, wrong decisions week in week out could cause the club Premier League status, the stakes are so high that video evidence will come into force.

Question 3.
What has been your most memorable professional moment and your most embarrassing personal moment?
Receiving my PFA players player of the year award in 1996 and also making my England debut.

Question 4.
If you could change any of the rules in football what would it be?
Too many changes have accrued in football over recent years, I'd like things to be left alone for a while.

Question 5.
You're playing in the cup final. It's 0-0 in the 89th minute. You're tackled by a defender in the penalty box. Would you think about taking a dive to get a penalty?
Too many cameras around you'd never get away with it. You'd be called a cheat for the rest of your life.

Question 6.
Do you have an alternative career plan for the day when you retire from professional football?
Nothing planned as yet. But the older I get the more I think about it.

Question 7.
What has been your funniest experience when travelling with your team?
Not printable!

Question 8.
Who would you most like to have an Amstel Beer with in the hot tub with you after a big match?
Depends on the result. But normally after a match I'm so tired I don't want anyone in the tub with me.

Question 9.
What is the most outrageous thing you have ever bought?
Black and white stripped jacket which I never had the front to wear!

Question 10.
Would you agree with England's Ian Wright that the feeling of scoring a goal is better than sex?
I love scoring goals and when I do score it's a great feeling, but better than sex? (Come on).

Alex Ferguson

MANAGER MANCHESTER UNITED FOOTBALL CLUB

Question 1.
Which football manager do you respect the most and why?
Sir Matt Busby - he created the most famous football club in the world and John Steen he had a vision no one could match.

Question 2.
How do you feel about the introduction of video evidence and reversible decisions during and after the match?
Very difficult particularly during winter.

Question 3.
What has been your most memorable professional moment and your most embarrassing personal moment?
I have had many great moments, winning the Championship and two European Cup winners cups.

Question 4.
If you could change any of the rules in football what would it be?
Offside - attackers are always penalised and defender's are given benefit of doubt - this is wrong .

Question 5.
You're playing in the cup final. It's 0 - 0 in the 89th minute. You're tackled by a defender in the penalty box. Would you think about taking a dive to get a penalty?
Only if contact was made and it was stopping your attempt to score.

Question 6.
Do you have an alternative career plan for the day when you retire from professional football?
Not at the moment as I want to remain in football as long as possible.

Question 7.
What has been your funniest experience when travelling with your team?
Usually when the players put a comedy video on. I don't particularly like silly videos and I threaten to destroy them.

Question 8.
Who would you most like to have an Amstel Beer with in the hot tub with you after a big match?
No Comment.

Question 9.
What is the most outrageous thing you have ever bought?
A check suit about 25 years ago, it was a bet.

Question 10.
Would you agree with England's Ian Wright that the feeling of scoring a goal is better than sex?
No Comment

Charlie George

EX-ARSENAL AND ENGLAND

Question 1.
Which football manager do you respect the most and why?
Arsene Wenger, for a French man to come to this country and put across his aspect of the game, and win the double when he is still in his learning years at the club has got to be well respected.

Question 2.
How do you feel about the introduction of video evidence and reversible decisions during and after the match?
I think you have got to study certain aspect of video evidence especially some of the referees decisions, we keep going on about the players but we have to look at the referees as well. It would be like an American football game, where the game actually last an hour and finishes four hours later. I think it will be introduced because there is so much money involved in the game especially for disallowed goals where the ball has travelled over the line and penalties.

Question 3.
What has been your most memorable professional moment and your most embarrassing personal moment?
The goal that clinched the double for Arsenal in 1971, scoring the winning goal at Wembley. I played in a friendly at Oxford one day I was caught short and I had to run off but I don't think they really missed me because I was playing that bad. I played for Derby at Middlesbrough many years ago, I scored an own goal.

Question 4.
If you could change any of the rules in football what would it be?
To make the game more attractive, 35 yard line.

Question 5.
You're playing in the cup final. It's 0-0 in the 89th minute. You're tackled by a defender in the penalty box. Would you think about taking a dive to get a penalty?
No I don't think so, I'd leave that to the European players. I don't agree with that. I'm not a lover of people cheating in the game, you're not cheating the opposing team you're cheating the public.

Question 6.
Did you have an alternative career plan for the day when you retired from professional football?
Yes, drinking as much beer as I could to keep the landlord very wealthy. Never thought about it.

Question 7.
What has been your funniest experience when travelling with your team?

When I was at Derby the assistant manager Frank Blandstone, his passport had gone missing or got lost, or taken or thrown away by one of the players whoever, we actually got through to the passport area and then decided to turn around and had to stay another two or three days in Iran which is not the best place in the world to be and come home a couple of days later.

Question 8.
Who would you most like to have an Amstel Beer with in the hot tub with you after a big match?

I'm divorced now, but I would have to say my ex-wife

Question 9.
What is the most outrageous thing you have ever bought?

Flared jeans with different colours on them.

Question 10.
Would you agree with England's Ian Wright that the feeling of scoring a goal is better than sex?

Yes, no matter where you play, everyone wants to score a goal and in the right situation for about 30 seconds it could be better than sex. Hopefully the sex I have had lasted a little bit longer.

John Giles

EX LEEDS AND REPUBLIC OF IRELAND

Question 1.
Which football manager do you respect the most and why?
Arsene Wenger, because he brings an intelligence to the game that's been missing a long time. Arsenal won trophies before under George Graham, but using many of the same players, Wenger played a much more attractive style, and in winning the Double in 1997/98, Arsenal played absolutely brilliant stuff.

Question 2.
How do you feel about the introduction of video evidence and reversible decisions during and after the match?
I think it's bound to come, I think it's a good idea. Referees have been sacred cows who never admit to being wrong, if they do make a mistake they say they're only human. If the technology comes in and brings a new element of justice to the game, it should be done.

Question 3.
What has been your most memorable professional moment and your most embarrassing personal moment?
Playing my first international when only 18. Playing with players that I'd idolised only three years before from the terraces at Dalymount

Park. It's something I'll never forget. Being part of the Leeds side that lost to Sunderland in the 1973 FA Cup Final.

Question 4.
If you could change any of the rules in football what would it be?
I think Goalkeepers take too long to kick the ball out. If a goalie touches the ball, he should have to kick it from inside the penalty area. Goalkeepers dribbling outside the penalty area wastes too much time.

Question 5.
You're playing in the cup final. It's 0 - 0 in the 89th minute. You're tackled by a defender in the penalty box. Would you think about taking a dive to get a penalty?
If there was contact in the tackle and I could go down to get the penalty, I would go down. But I never did dive and never would. I think if you ask any professional, if contact was made would they go down, I think they would say yes.

Question 6.
Did you have an alternative career plan for the day when you retired from professional football?
No. I always thought I'd go into management and I wasn't qualified to do anything outside of football.

Question 7.
What has been your funniest experience when travelling with your team?
The movie "The Spy Who Came in From The Cold" was filmed in Dublin, where they built a replica Berlin Wall. One of the Irish Officials bought the replica so Joe Kinnear, Ray Tracey and myself phoned him up with German accents saying we wanted him to go on German television for a fee to explain to the German people how he had bought the wall.

Question 8.
Who would you most like to have an Amstel Beer with in the hot tub with you after a big match?
Jack Nicklaus - always a hero of mine. I liked his approach to the game and I think it would be a great opportunity to talk to him.

Question 9.
What is the most outrageous thing you have ever bought?
I went to Carmaby Street with my wife Ann once and I bought a matching shirt and tie set, both the same colour. I wore it in the Leeds dressing room, where it's fair to say it didn't go without comment.

Question 10.
Would you agree with England's Ian Wright that the feeling of scoring a goal is better than sex?
No.

Shay Given

REPUBLIC OF IRELAND

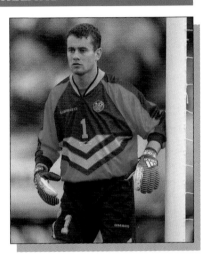

Question 1.
Which football manager do you respect the most and why?
Kenny Dalglish, because as a player he won everything and as a manager he also won a lot of trophies as well. He gave me my chance in the top flight.

Question 2.
How do you feel about the introduction of video evidence and reversible decisions during and after the match?
I would rather the game left the way it is, because it would slow the game down too much.

Question 3.
What has been your most memorable professional moment and your most embarrassing personal moment?
Making my international debut. The goal I conceeded against Dion Dublin last year.

Question 4.
If you could change any of the rules in football what would it be?
I would change the six second rule for goalkeepers.

Question 5.
You're playing in the cup final. It's 0 - 0 in the 89th minute. You're tackled by a defender in the penalty box. Would you think about taking a dive to get a penalty?
I would never be up that far!

Question 6.
Do you have an alternative career plan for the day when you retire from professional football?
I would like to stay involved with football in some manner.

Question 7.
What has been your funniest experience when travelling with your team?
Last year before the FA Cup semi final we forgot Temuri Ketsbia in the hotel. Looking back it was quite funny because it was such an important game.

Question 8.
Who would you most like to have an Amstel Beer with in the hot tub with you after a big match?
Tyra Banks

Question 9.
What is the most outrageous thing you have ever bought?
Some Lingerie!

Question 10.
Would you agree with England's Ian Wright that the feeling of scoring a goal is better than sex?
No!

Alan Gough

SHELBOURNE FOOTBALL CLUB

Question 1.
Which football manager do you respect the most and why?
Alex Ferguson. I respect the man the way he has totally believed Manchester United. At the beginning of his reign at Old Trafford there were cat calls for his head when things were not going well. However, not in Europe but the world Manchester United have put British football on the map.

Question 2.
How do you feel about the introduction of video evidence and reversible decisions during and after the match?
Football is now a business peoples livelihood. Careers are at stake. Roughly I believe it is worth an extra 9 million pounds to stay in the Premiership. So we have to follow the example of cricket with the video replay. I personally do not have a problem with this.

Question 3.
What has been your most memorable professional moment and your most embarrassing personal moment?
Making my league debut at 19 for Fulham. Being sent off in a domestic cup final here in Ireland.

Question 4.
If you could change any of the rules in football what would it be?
Speaking as a goalkeeper I find the new six second rule can become quite annoying.

Question 5.

FOUNDED 1895

You're playing in the cup final. It's 0-0 all in the 89th minute. You're tackled by a defender in the penalty box.
Would you think about taking a dive to get a penalty?
No, because as a rule we are honest people this side of the world and a clear conscience is a soft pillow.

Question 6.

Do you have an alternative career plan for the day when you retire from professional football?
I am a semi professional footballer and I also have a full-time career working for wider services here in the Republic of Ireland, selling Traco products to the car industry.

Question 7.

What has been your funniest experience when travelling with your team?
We were staying in a hotel on a Friday night where their was a disco on and our manager at the time went downstairs dressed in a towel only and lied down on the seats in front of reception and refused to go to bed until the music stopped. Not a pretty sight Mr. Murphy

Question 8.

Who would you most like to have an Amstel Beer with in the hot tub with you after a big match?
The league representative presenting us with the league trophy.

Question 9.

What is the most outrageous thing you have ever bought?
When I was younger pink T-Shirt with socks to match.

Question 10.

Would you agree with England's Ian Wright that the feeling of scoring a goal is better than sex?
Again as a goalkeeper I can't complain, but reading the newspapers it's good to see Ian getting plenty of practice at both!

Danny Granville

LEEDS UNITED FOOTBALL CLUB

Question 1.
Which football manager do you respect the most and why?
Glen Hoddle, for all the stick he has taken and that he has stuck to his guns.

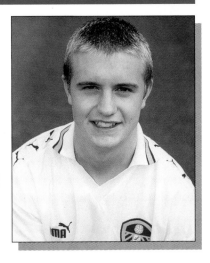

Question 2.
How do you feel about the introduction of video evidence and reversible decisions during and after the match?
It will help with certain decisions.

Question 3.
What has been your most memorable professional moment and your most embarrassing personal moment?
Cup Winners Cup with Chelsea. I went bowling and slipped because I was so bad at bowling.

Question 4.
If you could change any of the rules in football what would it be?
Tackle from behind. Challenging the goalkeeper, they are too protected.

Question 5.
You're playing in the cup final. It's 0-0 in the 89th minute. You're tackled by a defender in the penalty box. Would you think about taking a dive to get a penalty?
Yes!

Question 6.
Do you have an alternative career plan for the day when you retire from professional football?
Yes, maybe to be a manager, but see what happens, might be a beach bum instead!

Question 7.
What has been your funniest experience when travelling with your team? Loads! Martinique with Chelsea.
Playing Ching Chang and who ever lost had to walk back naked from the beach to the hotel. I went the wrong way, so I had a long walk.

Question 8.
Who would you most like to have an Amstel Beer with in the hot tub with you after a big match?
Natalie Imbruglia, Anna Friel, Gwyneth Paltrow, Eleanor Christianson, Sharpie, Lee Bowyer and Christy, Sharpie's mate, as he sounds fun.

Question 9.
What is the most outrageous thing you have ever bought?
My first Ford. That I wrote off and then gave it to my brother to fix.

Question 10.
Would you agree with England's Ian Wright that the feeling of scoring a goal is better than sex?
Yes, sometimes it all depends who I am with!

Eddie Gray

COACH LEEDS UNITED FOOTBALL CLUB

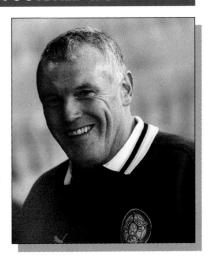

Question 1.
Which football manager do you respect the most and why?
Don Revie. He was a great manager and a great man. A big influence on my football career.

Question 2.
How do you feel about the introduction of video evidence and reversible decisions during and after the match?
Don't agree with it.

Question 3.
What has been your most memorable professional moment and your most embarrassing personal moment?
Winning the first League Championship for Leeds, 1st championship they won.

Question 4.
If you could change any of the rules in football what would it be?
Wouldn't change any.

Question 5.
You're playing in the cup final. It's 0-0 in the 89th minute. You're tackled by a defender in the penalty box. Would you think about taking a dive to get a penalty?
I would try and kid the referee.

Question 6.
Did you have an alternative career plan for the day when you retired from playing professional football?
I have retired and now I am coaching.

Question 7.
What has been your funniest experience when travelling with your team?
I have had a few but I wouldn't like to mention them!

Question 8.
Who would you most like to have an Amstel Beer with in the hot tub with you after a big match?
My wife. If you believe that you will believe anything!

Question 9.
What is the most outrageous thing you have ever bought?
A pair of black & white platform shoes in the 70's that looked like a chequer board. But they were very fashionable.

Question 10.
Would you agree with England's Ian Wright that the feeling of scoring a goal is better than sex?
No, he is talking a load of rubbish.

John Gregory

MANAGER ASTON VILLA FOOTBALL CLUB

Question 1.
Which football manager do you respect the most and why?
Alex Ferguson, because his record of success is without doubt the best in modern day football.

Question 2.
How do you feel about the introduction of video evidence and reversible decisions during and after the match?
Only during games!!

Question 3.
What has been your most memorable professional moment and your most embarrassing personal moment?
Representing my country and losing my job as manager of Portsmouth in 1990.

Question 4.
If you could change any of the rules in football what would it be?
None.

Question 5.
You're playing in the cup final. It's 0 - 0 in the 89th minute. You're tackled by a defender in the penalty box. Would you think about taking a dive to get a penalty?
Yes! Without doubt.

Question 6.
Do you have an alternative career plan for the day when you retire from professional football?
NO.

Question 7.
What has been your funniest experience when travelling with your team?
Football has always been a laugh a minute.

Question 8.
Who would you most like to have an Amstel Beer with in the hot tub with you after a big match?
Kate Peirson - B 52's

Question 9.
What is the most outrageous thing you have ever bought?
A pair of Gucci loafers in 1978, when they cost 2 weeks housekeeping!

Question 10.
Would you agree with England's Ian Wright that the feeling of scoring a goal is better than sex?
No.

Paul Hall

COVENTRY CITY FOOTBALL CLUB

Question 1.
Which football manager do you respect the most and why?
Alex Ferguson, because he is the most successful and he believes in what he does.

Question 2.
How do you feel about the introduction of video evidence and reversible decisions during and after the match?
I don't agree because it spoils the game and would create even more arguments after matches and peoples opinions would differ by an even wider margin than now. Only in desperate and obvious situations would I agree with it.

Question 3.
What has been your most memorable professional moment and your most embarrassing personal moment?
Most memorable, becoming a professional footballer at the basement of the football league, and then representing my country in the World Cup 10 years later.

Question 4.
If you could change any of the rules in football what would it be?
The offside trap. I would play the season in the summer.

Question 5.
You're playing in the cup final. It's 0 - 0 in the 89th minute. You're tackled by a defender in the penalty box. Would you think about taking a dive to get a penalty?
Yes. I would think about it.

Question 6.
Do you have an alternative career plan for the day when you retire from professional football?
I would hope to become a coach by then.

Question 7.
What has been your funniest experience when travelling with your team?
No Comment.

Question 8.
Who would you most like to have an Amstel Beer with in the hot tub with you after a big match?
No Comment.

Question 9.
What is the most outrageous thing you have ever bought?
The England Teams 1982 World Cup Song. "We'll Get It Right". I don't know what was going through my greasy head at the time.

Question 10.
Would you agree with England's Ian Wright that the feeling of scoring a goal is better than sex?
No. But it comes close.

Bryan Hamilton

DIRECTOR OF FOOTBALL - NORWICH CITY

Question 1.
Which football manager do you respect the most and why?
Bobby Robson, basically because I spent so much time with him. Not only was he successful in the UK but in Europe also.

Question 2.
How do you feel about the introduction of video evidence and reversible decisions during and after the match?
We have just got to accept that it is part of football now. TV is very much a part of the senior game and that TV evidence can be used for both referees and players, make the game fairer. Like everything else there is good and bad in it.

Question 3.
What has been your most memorable professional moment and your most embarrassing personal moment?
It's hard to say when you have been in the game for almost 35 years, what you can say is that the game is fantastic and I've been fortunate to play in a League Cup Final, FA Cup Finals, I've been playing at International level and all the European competitions. If I was to choose one, I'd have to say to captain your country is a fantastic feeling. We were sitting around a table last night with the lads, and we

were trying to pick out our most embarrassing moment, one of mine was going back in time, and I laugh about it myself now. As a young 15 year old I was signed and I'd gone from nobody knowing me to a lot of people knowing me in the town and my friend Tom Wilson and I used to go to the International matches together. It was a pound in, I was 5ft 5", he was a tall boy and I used to jump over the wall and he would pay and then we'd split it. And I was walking to a game in Windsor Park one day and a young kid came up to me and said "Are you Bryan Hamilton?" I said yes, we started talking and he said "Could you lift us over Bryan?" and I said "I'll be lifted over myself soon!"

Question 4.
If you could change any of the rules in football what would it be?
Basically what has been taken away is the common sense rule for referees. It's become so regimented, they're instructed to do so many things. I'd like to see it brought back.

Question 5.
You're playing in the cup final. It's 0-0 in the 89th minute. You're tackled by a defender in the penalty box. Would you think about taking a dive to get a penalty?
I wouldn't take a dive because I think that's unfair and you'd try encouraging young players not to abuse the rules and regulations. If it happens it happens.

Question 6.
Do you have an alternative career plan for the day when you retire from professional football?
Not really I've always been interested in sport and anything to do with people. I'm a people person. I'm lucky to live my life and work in the sporting world.

Question 7.
What has been your funniest experience when travelling with your team?
Generally the dressing room, it's always a real pleasure because there is always someone there with a great sense of humour, when your sitting with people and travelling with them, there is always some humorous event. Not one jumps out at me.

Question 8.
Who would you most like to have an Amstel Beer with in the hot tub with you after a big match?
I'd be very happy to have one with my wife.

Question 9.
What is the most outrageous thing you have ever bought?
I think my kids would say that some of my clothes are outrageous because I'm quite conservative with my dress. When we were younger (a hundred years ago) we used to buy all kinds of bits and pieces, maybe a Russian fur hat!

Question 10.
Would you agree with England's Ian Wright that the feeling of scoring a goal is better than sex?
No Comment!

Peter Hanrahan

BOHEMIANS FOOTBALL CLUB

Question 1.

Which football manager do you respect the most and why?
Joe Kinnear (Wimbledon) because of his ability to keep a club in the premiership with very little money.

Question 2.

How do you feel about the introduction of video evidence and reversible decisions during and after the match?
In favour during a match but not after.

Question 3.

What has been your most memorable professional moment and your most embarrassing personal moment?
Winning league medals 1991. Getting the ball in mid-region trying to block a shot (for all the crowd to see!)

Question 4.

If you could change any of the rules in football what would it be?
Offside - make it not apply.

Question 5.
You're playing in the cup final. It's 0 - 0 in the 89th minute. You're tackled by a defender in the penalty box. Would you think about taking a dive to get a penalty?
Yes of course.

Question 6.
Do you have an alternative career plan for the day when you retire from professional football?
Yes, investment analysis.

Question 7.
What has been your funniest experience when travelling with your team?
Roddy Collins jogging (to the rocky music) in front of the team van before his brother Steve Collins world title fight. (He was in the middle of the road drunk and pretending to be fighting ??? Rocky).

Question 8.
Who would you most like to have an Amstel Beer with in the hot tub with you after a big match?
Pamela Anderson.

Question 9.
What is the most outrageous thing you have ever bought?
A wedding ring - never thought I would.

Question 10.
Would you agree with England's Ian Wright that the feeling of scoring a goal is better than sex?
Yes

Jimmy Hasselbank

LEEDS UNITED FOOTBALL CLUB

Question 1.
Which football manager do you respect the most and why?
Louis Vangaal - Manager Barcelona. Because I like him.

Question 2.
How do you feel about the introduction of video evidence and reversible decisions during and after the match?
Not good, because there is a referee and he can see things.

Question 3.
What has been your most memorable professional moment and your most embarrassing personal moment?
Playing for Holland in the 1998 World Cup. When I head butted Keith Curl!

Question 4.
If you could change any of the rules in football what would it be?
No, I like them all.

Question 5.
You're playing in the cup final. It's 0 - 0 in the 89th minute. You're tackled by a defender in the penalty box. Would you think about taking a dive to get a penalty?
Yes, most definitely.

Question 6.
Do you have an alternative career plan for the day when you retire from professional football?
Not yet I am too young.

Question 7.
What has been your funniest experience when travelling with your team?
Getting stuck in the lift in Leeds Bradford airport!

Question 8.
Who would you most like to have an Amstel Beer with in the hot tub with you after a big match?
Only my girlfriend.

Question 9.
What is the most outrageous thing you have ever bought?
BMW 840

Question 10.
Would you agree with England's Ian Wright that the feeling of scoring a goal is better than sex?
More or less! But it all depends on who you are having sex with!!

John Hendrie

MANAGER BARNSLEY FOOTBALL CLUB

Question 1.
Which football manager do you respect the most and why?
Alex Ferguson - has been a success wherever he has managed.

Question 2.
How do you feel about the introduction of video evidence and reversible decisions during and after the match?
I don't agree with it.

Question 3.
What has been your most memorable professional moment and your most embarrassing personal moment?
Most memorable: My 5 promotions. Most embarrassing: Nothing springs to mind!

Question 4.
If you could change any of the rules in football what would it be?
Sending off goalkeepers for bringing the striker down. A penalty is sufficient.

Question 5.
You're playing in the cup final. It's 0 - 0 in the 89th minute. You're tackled by a defender in the penalty box. Would you think about taking a dive to get a penalty?
No. Well I don't think so.

Question 6.
Do you have an alternative career plan for the day when you retire from professional football?
No. 99% of footballers don't.

Question 7.
What has been your funniest experience when travelling with your team?
I was left behind when I missed the team bus home.

Question 8.
Who would you most like to have an Amstel Beer with in the hot tub with you after a big match?
Don't tell my wife. Claudia Schiffer.

Question 9.
What is the most outrageous thing you have ever bought?
I've a few dodgey suits.

Question 10.
Would you agree with England's Ian Wright that the feeling of scoring a goal is better than sex?
It depends on who the goals against.

Colin Hendry

RANGERS FOOTBALL CLUB

Question 1.
Which football manager do you respect the most and why?
Kenny Dalglish - Won every domestic honour as a player and manager. Plus everything in Europe as well. Also had the honour of being my manager for $3^{1/2}$ years.

Question 2.
How do you feel about the introduction of video evidence and reversible decisions during and after the match?
Possibly the way the game will go, but really decisions must be made within 90 minutes, or the length of the match.

Question 3.
What has been your most memorable professional moment and your most embarrassing personal moment?
Winning the Premier League in '95 with Blackburn and captaining my country Scotland. Knocking in an own goal in '88 in a 2nd division match for Blackburn Rovers -v- Oxford

Question 4.
If you could change any of the rules in football what would it be?
Revert back to passing the ball back to the keeper.

Question 5.
You're playing in the cup final. It's 0 - 0 in the 89th minute. You're tackled by a defender in the penalty box. Would you think about taking a dive to get a penalty?
No.

Question 6.
Do you have an alternative career plan for the day when you retire from professional football?
Yes, to try coaching then management - Why? Because I will probably always wonder what it is like.

Question 7.
What has been your funniest experience when travelling with your team?
Leaving Tim Flowers at the hotel at 1 o'clock when we were about to play Everton at 3 o'clock!

Question 8.
Who would you most like to have an Amstel Beer with in the hot tub with you after a big match?
Demi Moore - maybe get a massage as well!!!

Question 9.
What is the most outrageous thing you have ever bought?
I've had some tartan suits made, which a lot of people reckon are outrageous!

Question 10.
Would you agree with England's Ian Wright that the feeling of scoring a goal is better than sex?
I can't agree because the last 3 seasons I've scored one a season. No chance!

Gordon Hill

EX-MANCHESTER UNITED

Question 1.
Which football manager do you respect the most and why?
I respect most of the managers because they have such a tough job they have to do. Tommy Doherty, Don Reevey, Robson, Venables & Ron Greenwood.

Question 2.
How do you feel about the introduction of video evidence and reversible decisions during and after the match?
I still think football should not be put down to video evidence, if a decision is made we just have to make sure that the referees and the officials are more aware of what is happening with the new rules. I find that there is a new rule every year. It's very frustrating when you get officials that can't interpret the rules very cleverly and now players are actually diving and referees aren't giving any card then the referees get reprimanded for not giving enough cards. There are far too many cards going around the game at the moment for things that can be handled with common sense.

Question 3.
What has been your most memorable professional moment and your most embarrassing personal moment?
Being signed as a professional player, being signing with United. 1975, 1976 FA Cup Finals were great. Substituted at Wembley, not really

embarrassed but more disappointed, having to walk from one side of Wembley to the touch line and then walking off with so many people looking at you.

Question 4.
If you could change any of the rules in football what would it be?
One rule leads to another rule, so it would be difficult, probably not to bring in any new rules.

Question 5.
You're playing in the cup final. It's 0-0 all in the 89th minute. You're tackled by a defender in the penalty box. Would you think about taking a dive to get a penalty?
No. Never, never taken a dive, that is something that we have got to start outlawing. It has started creeping into our game, and I think it has a lot to do with the foreign imports that we have got coming in and the younger players are watching it. I would never fall for the sake of falling.

Question 6.
Did you have an alternative career plan for the day when you retired from professional football?
I was an apprentice paten maker in wood. I'm now in the media, but I learnt my trade. If I hadn't been a footballer I would have been a wood carver, I love working with wood.

Question 7.
What has been your funniest experience when travelling with your team?
On our way to Wembley for the cup final, in the United coach, red seats etc. On the way down going to the hotel a food fight broke out on the M1! When we got off the bus everyone was covered in food and the bus was a mess!

**Who would you most like to have an Amstel Beer with in the
hot tub with you after a big match?**
Sandra Bullock, top of the agenda.

Question 9.
What is the most outrageous thing you have ever bought?
A pair of flares about 25 inches wide, if the wind got up them I could
have flown from Manchester to London in about half an hour!

Question 10.
**Would you agree with England's Ian Wright that the feeling of
scoring a goal is better than sex?**
Definitely, Wrighty scored a few beauties. It's nothing you can really
explain, like goosebumps, sex is over in one minute at least with a
goal they remember that!

100

Denis Irwin

REPUBLIC OF IRELAND

Question 1.
Which football manager do you respect the most and why?
I respect all football managers, but the last two I've had at club level, Joe Royle and Alex Ferguson have impressed me the most. Alex Ferguson because of his dedication and desire to succeed and Joe Royle because of the way he handled his players

Question 2.
How do you feel about the introduction of video evidence and reversible decisions during and after the match?
I am not in favour of video evidence or any decisions being reversed. The game of football is well kept alone, in it's present state there's enough controversy in football already without adding to it. Has video evidence solved the 1966 World Cup Final goal, i.e. did it or didn't it cross the goal line.

Question 3.
What has been your most memorable professional moment and your most embarrassing personal moment?
Fortunately I've had plenty of memorable moments in football, signing of Leeds and playing for them and also signing for Manchester United and winning trophies. Beating Barcelona in 1991 ECWC, winning the League after the club waited 26 years were two great moments in club football. Playing in the World Cup Finals with Ireland in USA 1994. Scoring an own goal playing for Leeds against Newcastle.

Question 4.
If you could change any of the rules in football what would it be?
As I've said before, football is best left as it is.

Question 5.
You're playing in the cup final. It's 0 - 0 in the 89th minute. You're tackled by a defender in the penalty box. Would you think about taking a dive to get a penalty?
I wouldn't even think about it. I'd just do it. For example look at page 20 of the book "Hoping for Heroes".

Question 6.
Do you have an alternative career plan for the day when you retire from professional football?
Not at present. I wouldn't like to stay in the game as coach or manager, but there are other avenues opening up all the time.

Question 7.
What has been your funniest experience when travelling with your team?
There are too many to mention and most of them would be unprintable anyway!

Question 8.
Who would you most like to have an Amstel Beer with in the hot tub with you after a big match?
Jennifer Aniston from Friends.

Question 9.
What is the most outrageous thing you have ever bought?
I once bought a multi-coloured jacket by Kenzo, but have never worn it. It's just not me.

Question 10.
Would you agree with England's Ian Wright that the feeling of scoring a goal is better than sex?
No!

Darren Jackson

CELTIC FOOTBALL CLUB

Question 1.
Which football manager do you respect the most and why?
Alex Ferguson of Manchester United. He was probably only one game away from the sack at the club a few years ago, yet he still believed in himself and completely turned things around. He also brought a lot of good young players through the ranks and turned them into stars, showing that it can be done in this country.

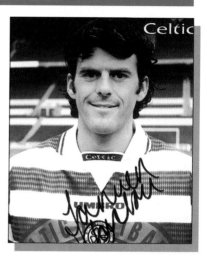

Question 2.
How do you feel about the introduction of video evidence and reversible decisions during and after the match?
I think for red card decisions it's good, then if the referee can look at the incident he can check if it's the right one and reverse it. It's not going to help the players at the time, but it's a good idea. As for during the game, no way. For offside decisions, etc. it would just take forever and it could end up like cricket with players standing about for ages waiting on decisions.

Question 3.

What has been your most memorable professional moment and your most embarrassing personal moment?
The most memorable moment has to be winning the 1997/98 League Championship with Celtic. Standing on that podium lifting the league trophy will take some beating. As for embarrassing moments, well I just don't have them!!

Question 4.

If you could change any of the rules in football what would it be?
I don't think I would change any, some, like offside, people may want to change as they would think it would open up the game a bit, but it would just be ridiculous, too open. I would however change one rule - no referee should be allowed to give any bad decisions against me!

Question 5.

You're playing in the cup final. It's 0 - 0 in the 89th minute. You're tackled by a defender in the penalty box. Would you think about taking a dive to get a penalty?
This is a hard one - do I lie or cheat? Honestly, it would depend on how hard the defender tackled me. That's my diplomatic answer!

Question 6.

Do you have an alternative career plan for the day when you retire from professional football?
I don't just now at all. I'd like to stay in the game in some capacity - but I don't think I'd ever get the managers job at Celtic!

Question 7.
What has been your funniest experience when travelling with your team?
It wasn't with Celtic, but with Dundee United a few years ago. Everyone knew what a hard taskmaster the then boss Jim McLean was, and anyway, we were going through customs when you put your hand luggage through the scanner and the customs officer picked out his bag to search. He opened it up and brought out the biggest can of hairspray you have ever seen in your life, and the boys just could not stop laughing at all. It was hilarious and nothing since has beaten it.

Question 8.
Who would you most like to have an Amstel Beer with in the hot tub with you after a big match?
My girlfriend, Arlene.

Question 9.
What is the most outrageous thing you have ever bought?
Well, I've always liked clothes and it was, again, back in my Dundee United days, six or seven years ago. They were the most outrageous pair of white flares ever. I'm not exactly fat now, but I was even skinnier then and I thought they were the business at the time!

Question 10.
Would you agree with England's Ian Wright that the feeling of scoring a goal is better than sex?
Only people in football can experience the sensation of scoring a goal and I would have to agree with Ian Wright on this one....but sex isn't bad either, right enough!

Juninho

ATLETICO DE MADRID S.A.D.

Question 1.
Which football manager do you respect the most and why?
I don't have one in particular. Each one of those I have had in my football career brought something to my personal knowledge on and off the pitch. We footballers are human beings and I think that we can learn something new everyday.

Question 2.
How do you feel about the introduction of video evidence and reversible decisions during and after the match?
I hope that video evidence will never be introduced as it would alter the game. Football must remain a game and should not become a technological device on the pitch. Apart from that, we all know that you can bias any video sequel, which would not ethically be correct. One same incident seen from different angles or video excerpts could lead to different decisions. Nobody's perfect and let's protect the game!

Question 3.
What has been your most memorable professional moment and your most embarrassing personal moment?
Most memorable: To meet Pele. Most embarrassing: My repeated injuries, keeping me thus away from the football grounds for a long time (as last season and beginning of the current one).

Question 4.
If you could change any of the rules in football what would it be?
Replace the penalty shoot out session by a replay in order to decide the winners of an important challenge. The sudden death rule is inhuman and far from bringing something to football.

Question 5.
You're playing in the cup final. It's 0 - 0 in the 89th minute. You're tackled by a defender in the penalty box. Would you think about taking a dive to get a penalty?
I never dive or look for an advantage by cheating on any ref. Attacking football should be protected with harder rules but diving should also be punished.

Question 6.
Do you have an alternative career plan for the day when you retire from professional football?
Not yet. But maybe some business with football or teaching to youngsters.

Question 7.
What has been your funniest experience when travelling with your team?
That all our luggage, equipment and football boots did not arrive in time as there was a misunderstanding at the airport.

Question 8.
Who would you most like to have an Amstel Beer with in the hot tub with you after a big match?
No comment

Question 9.
What is the most outrageous thing you have ever bought?
A Car!

Question 10.
Would you agree with England's Ian Wright that the feeling of scoring a goal is better than sex?
Each time you score a goal you feel something very strong and unique. It is not an orgasm but it is indeed a feeling you enjoy a lot.

Roy Keane

REPUBLIC OF IRELAND

Question 1.
Which football manager do you respect the most and why?

Brian Clough and Alex Ferguson. First Brian Clough for giving me my chance in England and just learning from him every single day. Alex Ferguson for bringing me to a great club and watching in amazement the hunger he has for the game, considering everything he's won in the game.

Question 2.
How do you feel about the introduction of video evidence and reversible decisions during and after the match?

I don't really believe in it because I think if things go for you or against you in a game that things usually even themselves out over the course of a season

Question 3.
What has been your most memorable professional moment and your most embarrassing personal moment?

Most memorable, well I have to say I have been very fortunate in football, so to pick out one thing wouldn't be right. Most embarrassing, well I get quiet embarrassed losing a game, so that would be my answer.

Question 4.
If you could change any of the rules in football what would it be?
None of them.

Question 5.
You're playing in the cup final. It's 0 - 0 in the 89th minute. You're tackled by a defender in the penalty box. Would you think about taking a dive to get a penalty?
If it meant winning then yes!

Question 6.
Do you have an alternative career plan for the day when you retire from professional football?
No!

Question 7.
What has been your funniest experience when travelling with your team?
Too many to mention!

Question 8.
Who would you most like to have an Amstel Beer with in the hot tub with you after a big match?
Jennifer Aniston.

Question 9.
What is the most outrageous thing you have ever bought?
An expensive car.

Question 10.
Would you agree with England's Ian Wright that the feeling of scoring a goal is better than sex?
No!

Jeff Kenna

REPUBLIC OF IRELAND

Question 1.
Which football manager do you respect the most and why?
Alex Ferguson, the most successful manager of the 90's

Question 2.
How do you feel about the introduction of video evidence and reversible decisions during and after the match?
Not in favour of it. It would take the excitement out of the game. No continuous decisions. It would leave people with nothing to talk about!

Question 3.
What has been your most memorable professional moment and your most embarrassing personal moment?
Winning the League with Blackburn. Scoring an own goal at Manchester United.

Question 4.
If you could change any of the rules in football what would it be?
No offside.

Question 5.
You're playing in the cup final. It's 0 - 0 in the 89th minute. You're tackled by a defender in the penalty box. Would you think about taking a dive to get a penalty?
No!

Question 6.
Do you have an alternative career plan for the day when you retire from professional football?
No!

Question 7.
What has been your funniest experience when travelling with your team?
Having to travel back from a game with a window missing from the coach!

Question 8.
Who would you most like to have an Amstel Beer with in the hot tub with you after a big match?
My wife.

Question 9.
What is the most outrageous thing you have ever bought?
An expensive coat.

Question 10.
Would you agree with England's Ian Wright that the feeling of scoring a goal is better than sex?
No chance!

Dean Kiely

REPUBLIC OF IRELAND

Question 1.
Which football manager do you respect the most and why?
John Ward, my manager at York City. I respect him the most because he is the manager I learnt the most about football from.

Question 2.
How do you feel about the introduction of video evidence and reversible decisions during and after the match?
I feel that it will be introduced but I don't think you should be able to reverse decisions after the game.

Question 3.
What has been your most memorable professional moment and your most embarrassing personal moment?
Gaining promotion with Bury to the 1st division. Having a half eaten steak and kidney pie thrown at me and hitting me right in the face.

Question 4.
If you could change any of the rules in football what would it be?
Nothing.

Question 5.
You're playing in the cup final. It's 0 - 0 in the 89th minute. You're tackled by a defender in the penalty box. Would you think about taking a dive to get a penalty?
Yes!

Question 6.
Do you have an alternative career plan for the day when you retire from professional football?
Ideally I would like to stay involved in football in some capacity.

Question 7.
What has been your funniest experience when travelling with your team?
Travelling to a friendly we arrived an hour late after changing buses twice and finally arriving in a convoy of Taxi's!

Question 8.
Who would you most like to have an Amstel Beer with in the hot tub with you after a big match?
Girlfriend, Jenny McCarthy or Caprice!

Question 9.
What is the most outrageous thing you have ever bought?
Gymbody 8!

Question 10.
Would you agree with England's Ian Wright that the feeling of scoring a goal is better than sex?
No, he mustn't be doing it right!

Joe Kinear

MANAGER WIMBLEDON FOOTBALL CLUB

Question 1.
Which football manager do you respect the most and why?
Bill Nicholson & Eddie Baily of Spurs. I played under them for 12 years. I respect most managers in football, but that doesn't mean you have to like some of them. They are members of the "Funny Farm".

Question 2.
How do you feel about the introduction of video evidence and reversible decisions during and after the match?
I believe that the referee should have the choice to ask for video evidence if he is not sure about a crucial decision, e.g. penalty, ball crossing, goal lines.

Question 3.
What has been your most memorable professional moment and your most embarrassing personal moment?
I have been very lucky in this department. My first Cap for Ireland, my first cup final and my first European Cup Final. And luckily enough to have won them all. Too many embarrassing moments!

Question 4.
If you could change any of the rules in football what would it be?
I wouldn't, there are enough already being changed. We have a good product leave it alone.

Question 5.
You're playing in the cup final. It's 0 - 0 in the 89th minute. You're tackled by a defender in the penalty box. Would you think about taking a dive to get a penalty?

No way! And anybody who would ain't worth a toss!!
To cheat and deceive your fellow professional's should be a life ban!! That would put an end to it once and for all..

Question 6.
Do you have an alternative career plan for the day when you retire from professional football?

I want to still have my hair & sanity. I won't retire till I am 60! 15 years to go!! So I intend to enjoy every minute of the job. I love it.

Question 7.
What has been your funniest experience when travelling with your team?

Every Saturday and winning at Manchester United. I have a great bunch of players who are real pros, but also have got a sense of humour.

Question 8.
Who would you most like to have an Amstel Beer with in the hot tub with you after a big match?

"Jenny Pitman". Just think that way I would get the next Grand National Winner!

Question 9.
What is the most outrageous thing you have ever bought? "

Vinny Jones One of my best pals!

Question 10.
Would you agree with England's Ian Wright that the feeling of scoring a goal is better than sex?

I don't know, I haven't seen his Misses!!

Denis Law

EX MANCHESTER UNITED AND SCOTLAND

Question 1.
Which football manager do you respect the most and why?
Alex Ferguson, because he is Scottish!
Past manager - Sir Mat Busby, because
he was Scottish! Jock Stein, as above.
Bill Shankly - Ditto!

Question 2.
How do you feel about the introduction of video evidence and reversible decisions during and after the match?
Football has never been played under those conditions and shouldn't be changed.

Question 3.
What has been your most memorable professional moment and your most embarrassing personal moment?
Memorable: Playing for Scotland
Embarassing: Returning Gazpache soup, complaining it was cold!

Question 4.
If you could change any of the rules in football what would it be?
In World Cup games, have the penalties before the game so when you have to play extra time you would know exactly what you would have

to do in order to win the game. Therefore not reducing the game to penalties.

Question 5.
You're playing in the cup final. It's 0 - 0 in the 89th minute. You're tackled by a defender in the penalty box. Would you think about taking a dive to get a penalty?
Who do you think I am? Franny Lee!!!

Question 6.
Do you have an alternative career plan for the day when you retire from professional football?
Do you mean to tell me I've not retired yet!

Question 7.
What has been your funniest experience when travelling with your team?
When a Scottish player (not to be named) on a club tour to America. ordered cooly from the barman, "A large bourbon on the rocks, without the ice!". Classic.

Question 8.
Who would you most like to have an Amstel Beer with in the hot tub with you after a big match?
Besty, Nobby, Bobby, and all the lads!

Question 9.
What is the most outrageous thing you have ever bought?
A round of drinks!!

Question 10.
Would you agree with England's Ian Wright that the feeling of scoring a goal is better than sex?
Nice one!!!!

Mark Lawrenson

EX-LIVERPOOL AND REPUBLIC OF IRELAND

Question 1.
Which football manager do you respect the most and why?
Alex Ferguson, he put together an excellent team at Manchester United. He is one of those managers who when he took over the job he could have well and truly lost the job in the early stages if it weren't for the fact that they had a very strong chairman in Martin Edward's. Plus I think he has a little bit of everything, he has a hard streak, he is very tactically aware. He knows exactly what he's doing in the

transfer market. He is one of those people you would like to think you could have played for.

Question 2.
How do you feel about the introduction of video evidence and reversible decisions during and after the match?
Well, I don't think there could be reversible decisions after matches, I think once the referee blows the final whistle that's it. There could be reversible decisions regarding disciplinary measures. The thing about football is that it is played at a very fast pace, if we can come up with some kind of technical equipment that can say yes it was over the line, no it wasn't within a matter of 5/10 seconds then I think people would stand for it, if it would delay the game it wouldn't be a good thing.

Question 3.
What has been your most memorable professional moment and your most embarrassing personal moment?
The day I made my debut for Preston North End my home town club, I had watched them as a kid, my dad had played. I was 18 years old and I thought I had made it. There's been quite a few, probably something like scoring an own goal. I had three of my front teeth knocked out when I was 18 during a match.

Question 4.
If you could change any of the rules in football what would it be?
Teams loosing 10 yards for decent. When a team get a free kick and the opposition argue with the referee the offenders should be prosecuted by having the free kick move 10 yards further up the pitch (as in GAA).

Question 5.
You're playing in the cup final. It's 0 -0 all in the 89th minute. You're tackled by a defender in the penalty box. Would you think about taking a dive to get a penalty?
Yes, I think if you honestly ask this question to every professional footballer, I would find it very difficult for them not to say Yes.

Question 6.
Did you have an alternative career plan for the day when you retired from professional football?
No I didn't actually I wanted to be a cricketer as much as a footballer and then once I started playing football professionally there was no way I could go to cricket when I finished. I started management at Oxford, and I walked out because I didn't agree with what Mr. Maxwell was insisting that the club did so I have my career in media, so I was very fortunate that I never had to sit down and decided what am I going to do now.

Question 7.
What has been your funniest experience when travelling with your team?
Travelling with Ireland, playing in a place in Poland, we were there 3 or 4 days before we played the National team and the food wasn't great. Most of the boys had stomach upsets and coming back on the bus after the game Kevin O'Callaghan got caught short shall we say. We had all been given these nice little embroidered doilies with the Republic of Ireland and the date on them, well let me put it this way. We had no toilet roll there was nowhere we could stop, so everyone's free gift was utilised.

Question 8.
Who would you most like to have an Amstel Beer with in the hot tub with you after a big match?
Well it would have to be female obviously! Very difficult, Denise Van Outen.

Question 9.
What is the most outrageous thing you have ever bought?
Probably a BMW sports car, soft top, which you might think is not very outrageous. But when you already have a car, it spent most of the time in the garage. Certainly my second half thought it was outrageous.

Question 10.
Would you agree with England's Ian Wright that the feeling of scoring a goal is better than sex?
I didn't score that many goals, it can be similar but not quite as good.

Derek Lilley

LEEDS UNITED FOOTBALL CLUB

Question 1.
Which football manager do you respect the most and why?
Alan McGraw manager Morton. He gave me my first break.

Question 2.
How do you feel about the introduction of video evidence and reversible decisions during and after the match?
Agree up to a point.

Question 3.
What has been your most memorable professional moment and your most embarrassing personal moment?
Played against Celtic in quarter finals of Scottish Cup. I got my ear pierced when I was 16 and I didn't like needles. I felt faint and fell against a glass window and fainted, very embarrassing.

Question 4.
If you could change any of the rules in football what would it be?
From a strikers point of view the offside rule.

Question 5.
You're playing in the cup final. It's 0-0 in the 89th minute. You're tackled by a defender in the penalty box. Would you think about taking a dive to get a penalty?
Yes definitely.

Question 6.
Do you have an alternative career plan for the day when you retire from professional football?
I am a qualified engineer but I would like to have my own business one day.

Question 7.
What has been your funniest experience when travelling with your team?
When we went to USA, Lee Bowyer left his clock on British time, but anything with Lee Bowyer is funny.

Question 8.
Who would you most like to have an Amstel Beer with in the hot tub with you after a big match?
Liz Hurley, Gwyneth Paltrow and my wife Shona..

Question 9.
What is the most outrageous thing you have ever bought?
I bought a rubber waistcoat. I sweated terribly but I thought I looked great.

Question 10.
Would you agree with England's Ian Wright that the feeling of scoring a goal is better than sex?
At the moment, Yes. As my wife has just had a baby and I ain't getting any sex!

Rodney Marsh

EX MANCHESTER CITY & FULHAM

Question 1.
Which football manager do you respect the most and why?
Several, Alex Ferguson, Arsene Wenger and George Graham. Wenger, because he is very analitical, comes across as being very efficent in what he does, he manages in a style that is unique to him. He could become an even greater manager than he already is. Graham, I admire his single mindedness, he has the same approach no matter what he does, honest and has a lot of integrity Ferguson, probably the greatest manager we've had since Paisley.

Question 2.
How do you feel about the introduction of video evidence and reversible decisions during and after the match?
Only for goals, and you wouldn't change a decision after the game. If there is a camera on the goal line whether a ball crosses the line or not, that is the only reason and it should be done at the time, I would like to see that introduced.

Question 3.
What has been your most memorable professional moment and your most embarrassing personal moment?
There is so many, playing with the late great Bobby Moore at Fulham.

I will always treasure that and now he's dead, it means even more to me that I played with the greatest defender we ever had. Too many to name! When I threw away my League Cup loosers medal, in 1974 for Manchester City against Wolves and we lost. On the Monday afterward I rang the FA to see if I could get another one and they told me to Piss Off!

Question 4.
If you could change any of the rules in football what would it be?
Two rules, 35 yard line for off side. That would mean that a player wouldn't be off side until 35 yards from the goal. There would be a line on the pitch across both ends. It makes the game more wide open and it dictates that the linesman virtually he only has to run the line in the last 35 yards of the pitch and even he couldn't get that wrong! At the end of 90 mins in drawn matches, I would like to see the players in a shoot out from the 35 yard line where the player has 5 seconds to take a shot against the goalkeeper one on one. Therefore you always have a winner.

Question 5.
You're playing in the cup final. It's 0 - 0 in the 89th minute. You're tackled by a defender in the penalty box. Would you think about taking a dive to get a penalty?
Yes, I wouldn't even think about it.

Question 6.
Did you have an alternative career plan for the day when you retired from professional football?
No, I had no idea what I was going to do.

Question 7.
What has been your funniest experience when travelling with your team?
When George Best came in one night on a tour of Norway with Fulham, and we were rooming together George and I, we had to get

the 10am flight the next morning and George came into the hotel and asked for a wake up call and the concierge said "Certainly Mr. Best, What time?", George said "7:30". The concierge said "It's twenty to eight now!"

Question 8.
Who would you most like to have an Amstel Beer with in the hot tub with you after a big match?
Elle MacPherson, the most gourgeous woman in the world.

Question 9.
What is the most outrageous thing you have ever bought?
Classic Rolls Royce, 2 weeks ago!

Question 10.
Would you agree with England's Ian Wright that the feeling of scoring a goal is better than sex?
It's definatley in the top 2! Ian is a very outspoken young man and I have a lot of respect for Ian Wright.

Mick McCarthy

MANAGER REPUBLIC OF IRELAND

Question 1.
Which football manager do you respect the most and why?
Alex Ferguson, for all his success with Aberdeen and Manchester United.

Question 2.
How do you feel about the introduction of video evidence and reversible decisions during and after the match?
I think it would be a good idea as there is so much at stake in football now. And it would help the referees.

Question 3.
What has been your most memorable professional moment and your most embarrassing personal moment?
Playing in Rome for Ireland in Quarter Finals of World Cup 1990. Running onto the pitch in China and tripping up and going head over heels

Question 4.
If you could change any of the rules in football what would it be?
The five day call up rule for international players.

Question 5.
You're playing in the cup final. It's 0 - 0 in the 89th minute. You're tackled by a defender in the penalty box. Would you think about taking a dive to get a penalty?
No, I can't dive.

Question 6.
Do you have an alternative career plan for the day when you retire from professional football?
I've no intentions of retiring just yet. When I do I hope I'll be old enough not to worry about another career.

Question 7.
What has been your funniest experience when travelling with your team?
On tour in Japan one of the lads made reference to Japanese pilots bombing his Gran's chip shop, as a joke to a group of Japanese people sat in our hotel. Only to find out to his horror that they spoke better English than him!

Question 8.
Who would you most like to have an Amstel Beer with in the hot tub with you after a big match?
The Irish football team after qualifying for Euro 2000.

Question 9.
What is the most outrageous thing you have ever bought?
A Honda Pan European motorbike, outrageous but brilliant.

Question 10.
Would you agree with England's Ian Wright that the feeling of scoring a goal is better than sex?
No. He's obviously not doing it properly. Mind you I didn't score that many goals anyway. So it's just as well I don't agree.

Ali McCoist

KILMARNOCK FOOTBALL CLUB

Question 1.
Which football manager do you respect the most and why?
Walter Smith, he gave me an opportunity to get back on track when I was up against it with the press etc.

Question 2.
How do you feel about the introduction of video evidence and reversible decisions during and after the match?
It's good, so much is hinging on the game, players and referees make mistakes. Bad, because it's not going to be universal, only in big match game.

Question 3.
What has been your most memorable professional moment and your most embarrassing personal moment?
Scoring a hat trick for Rangers against Celtic in '84. Winning the Cup Final in Scotland, Cheltenham at the Gold Cup I had too many Guinness's, that night I walked into the room, into the en suite, went to the toilet then got into bed with two strangers! I was quite embarrassed the next morning, the couple were very good about it!

Question 4.
If you could change any of the rules in football what would it be?
Offside rule.

Question 5.
You're playing in the cup final. It's 0 - 0 in the 89th minute. You're tackled by a defender in the penalty box. Would you think about taking a dive to get a penalty?
Not even a wee bit! YES! But again I would probably be embarrassed the next morning!

Question 6.
Do you have an alternative career plan for the day when you retire from professional football?
No, because I'm scared!
All I know & do is football. I don't even want to think about it.

Question 7.
What has been your funniest experience when travelling with your team?
Flying to Madrid for the Euro Cup tie. We put one of the midfielders on the wrong plane to Barcelona! Only when the manager did a head count, he realised someone was missing.

Question 8.
Who would you most like to have an Amstel Beer with in the hot tub with you after a big match?
The Managing Director of Amstel Beer. So I could sweet talk him into giving me free Amstel Beer for the rest of my life!

Question 9.
What is the most outrageous thing you have ever bought?
Yamaha 125 drill bike! All I can do is look at it and sit on it. I'm scared of it, they go too fast!.

Question 10.
Would you agree with England's Ian Wright that the feeling of scoring a goal is better than sex?
No! Because he has scored better goals than me! I've had a couple of goals that were nearly at the tickly bit, but not better!

Malcom McDonald

EX NEWCASTLE & ARSENAL

Question 1.
Which football manager do you respect the most and why?
Quite a lot to choose from, I think at this moment in time, Alex Ferguson, the reasons being that, he has shown himself very capable. Created a very good youth team. He creates the bases from home grown talent and then buys in the icing on the cake.

Question 2.
How do you feel about the introduction of video evidence and reversible decisions during and after the match?
Into the world of hi-tech! When I was playing 1 in 15 of my goals were ever recorded, everything that goes on in the field is recorded now. The players are under a lot of scrutiny and referees as well, if the technology is there then I think it must be used to create a better game, but I don't agree with reversible decision's after the match.

Question 3.
What has been your most memorable professional moment and your most embarrassing personal moment?
Scoring my first goal for England at Wembley 1975 against West Germany, it was the 1st match Germany played after winning the world cup in 1974, we beat them 2-0, I scored the second goal. Playing for Arsenal against Red Star Belgrade in Singapore, at the end of 90 mins we

were 1-1 so we went into extra time. The temp was over 100⁰C, humidity 98%. I was running through with the ball, with just the goalkeeper to beat, and with it being so hot, the elastic on my shorts broke, and fell to my ankles and tripped me over in front of 50,000 people. I didn't score I was flat on my face.

Question 4.
If you could change any of the rules in football what would it be?
I would change the shirt tugging, if it is seen that a shirt is pulled then it's a fowl.

Question 5.
You're playing in the cup final. It's 0 - 0 in the 89th minute. You're tackled by a defender in the penalty box. Would you think about taking a dive to get a penalty?
No, it wouldn't cross my mind.

Question 6.
Did you have an alternative career plan for the day when you retired from professional football?
I had a business in Men's clothing while I was a player. It was my plan to concentrate on that when I retired from playing, it didn't get the adrenaline running and I found myself going into football management.

Question 7.
What has been your funniest experience when travelling with your team?
Travelling with the England side on way to a Wembley International against Cyprus, I scored five goals, the motorbike out-riders with the police, took us through Barnet in between the hotel and Wembley, the motorbikes went through a gateless gate area but the bus couldn't make it down and so we had to reverse on the grass and the wheels

got stuck in the mud. On the way to Wembley, the countries finest footballers and we all had to get out and push the bus out of the mud. We were all fighting for positions to make sure we weren't behind the wheel, the ones that didn't think about it got caught behind the wheel and finished up covered in mud from top to toe.

Question 8.
Who would you most like to have an Amstel Beer with in the hot tub with you after a big match?
Barbara Striesand, great personality, great voice.

Question 9.
What is the most outrageous thing you have ever bought?
I have to think about that one. The first sports car I ever had in the early 70's in it's first 10 months I only had it on the road for about 2 weeks, I had so much trouble with it. It was bright orange, huge clouds of black smoke coming out of it. The gear box feel out. One thing after another!

Question 10.
Would you agree with England's Ian Wright that the feeling of scoring a goal is better than sex?
Yeah, you don't get 15,000 people watching you having sex and cheering you on!

Leon Mckenzie

CRYSTAL PALACE FOOTBALL CLUB

Question 1.
Which football manager do you respect the most and why?
Alex Ferguson, because he knows what he's doing.

Question 2.
How do you feel about the introduction of video evidence and reversible decisions during and after the match?
Yes I think it would help a lot and then we could sort out the right decisions because most of them are wrong anyway.

Question 3.
What has been your most memorable professional moment and your most embarrassing personal moment?
My first goal for Crystal Palace, and I do not yet have an embarrassing moment, sorry to say.

Question 4.
If you could change any of the rules in football what would it be?
Scrap offside because there would be more goals for me.

Question 5.
You're playing in the cup final. It's 0 - 0 in the 89th minute. You're tackled by a defender in the penalty box. Would you think about taking a dive to get a penalty?
Yes!

Question 6.
Do you have an alternative career plan for the day when you retire from professional football?
Have my own business.

Question 7.
What has been your funniest experience when travelling with your team?
The last Pre Season, but I can't go into detail.

Question 8.
Who would you most like to have an Amstel Beer with in the hot tub with you after a big match?
Too tricky!

Question 9.
What is the most outrageous thing you have ever bought?
No comment.

Question 10.
Would you agree with England's Ian Wright that the feeling of scoring a goal is better than sex?
It's just as good but if I scored goals as much as I have sex, well things might change (joke) you can't beat scoring.

Alan McLoughlin

REPUBLIC OF IRELAND

Question 1.
Which football manager do you respect the most and why?
Alex Ferguson, for all he has achieved at Manchester United. A pressure job and he has produced the goods with silverware and young talent making the grade.

Question 2.
How do you feel about the introduction of video evidence and reversible decisions during and after the match?
A good idea, too much at stake nowadays.

Question 3.
What has been your most memorable professional moment and your most embarrassing personal moment?
Scoring the winning goal at Wembley 1990 Play off final for Swinden. My shorts pulled down in a packed room of people, just before the World Cup 1990, by John Byrne.

Question 4.
If you could change any of the rules in football what would it be?
When injured you have to leave the pitch, only to be waved back on ten seconds later!

Question 5.
You're playing in the cup final. It's 0 - 0 all in the 89th minute. You're tackled by a defender in the penalty box. Would you think about taking a dive to get a penalty?
Yes!

Question 6.
Do you have an alternative career plan for the day when you retire from professional football?
Yes!

Question 7.
What has been your funniest experience when travelling with your team?
Not realising I had a golf ball in the bottom of my Guinness pint, twenty minutes later, it hit my nose with my last swig! The pub rocked with laughter, it took month's to live it down.

Question 8.
Who would you most like to have an Amstel Beer with in the hot tub with you after a big match?
No Comment.

Question 9.
What is the most outrageous thing you have ever bought?
A citrus green Mondeo SRI, nice car shame about the colour, a bad mistake.

Question 10.
Would you agree with England's Ian Wright that the feeling of scoring a goal is better than sex?
No!

Ian McNeil

CHIEF SCOUT, EX-PLAYER, COACH & MANAGER. HAS BEEN IN FOOTBALL FOR 50 YEARS THIS YEAR. LEEDS UNITED FOOTBALL CLUB

Question 1.

Which football manager do you respect the most and why?

George Graham, he has won Championship, his man management is good. He does all the coaching, he is the best coach I have seen in a lifetime in football.

Question 2.

How do you feel about the introduction of video evidence and reversible decisions during and after the match?

Anything that will improve the mistakes referees and linesmen make will no doubt better our game. Managers can lose their jobs on bad decisions by officials.

Question 3.

What has been your most memorable professional moment and your most embarrassing personal moment?

Scoring a hat-trick for Leicester City -v- Sunderland in the English 1st Division. After scoring on my league debut for Aberdeen as a 17 year old. I was left out of the 1st team the following week. The experienced players told me to speak to the boss. I asked the boss why I was in the second team. He replied "Because I haven't got a third team!!!" The rest of the team killed themselves laughing.

Question 4.
If you could change any of the rules in football what would it be?
I would change the offside rule to take place only inside a line 18 yards from the goal.

Question 5.
You're playing in the cup final. It's 0 -0 all in the 89th minute. You're tackled by a defender in the penalty box. Would you think about taking a dive to get a penalty?
It is a spur of the moment situation. But I do not think I would continuously take a dive.

Question 6.
Do you have an alternative career plan for the day when you retire from professional football?
I made provisions before I took up full time football, and I am a qualified engineering draughtsman, but after nearly 50 years in football I don't think I will be going back to engineering.

Question 7.
What has been your funniest experience when travelling with your team?
On a tour of Germany. We were travelling down the Rheime Valley, the night before we had a few drinks. One or two of the lads needed to relieve themselves. One player went behind the bus and took longer to finish. The coach left without him and it was 10 miles or so before it was discovered.

Question 8.
Who would you most like to have an Amstel Beer with in the hot tub with you after a big match?
Our two laundry ladies (My wife won't see this, will she?)

Question 9.
What is the most outrageous thing you have ever bought?
Bought a new car, had it delivered and failed driving test the day before!

Question 10.
Would you agree with England's Ian Wright that the feeling of scoring a goal is better than sex?
As an ex-striker, it would depend on the quality of the goal and the quality of the sex. You can get some tap-in goals and some crackers, same with sex!!

Alex Miller

MANAGER ABERDEEN FOOTBALL CLUB

Question 1.
Which football manager do you respect the most and why?
Any football manager that works wonders with no real financial support and produces good teams.

Question 2.
How do you feel about the introduction of video evidence and reversible decisions during and after the match?
The game is played at high speed and I believe it would be advantageous to have video evidence like cricket to determine a goal if there is doubt.

Question 3.
What has been your most memorable professional moment and your most embarrassing personal moment?
Two personal moments winning my first senior cup medal, Rangers - v- Celtic S.L.C. 1969/70. Manager of Hibernian FC in 1990/91 winning Skol Cup -v- Dunfermline Ath. Conducting myself improperly in a match, Hibernian -v- Dun. United with the opposition coach which was viewed by the TV cameras and I regret my behaviour to this day.

Question 4.
If you could change any of the rules in football what would it be?
If a player feigns injury on the judgement of the referee then he should be sent off, it would definitely clean up the game.

Question 5.
You're playing in the cup final. It's 0 - 0 in the 89th minute. You're tackled by a defender in the penalty box. Would you think about taking a dive to get a penalty?
No, for two reasons. As a player I was very rarely in the opposition penalty box and and I was never good at diving both on the field of play and in a swimming pool!

Question 6.
Do you have an alternative career plan for the day when you retire from professional football?
No I hope that day is still a long way off.

Question 7.
What has been your funniest experience when travelling with your team?
On a small plane in Scandonavia when all the players put on a life jacket and awakened a sleeping team mate seconds before landing at Malmo Airport with the runway positioned with water on both sides.

Question 8.
Who would you most like to have an Amstel Beer with in the hot tub with you after a big match?
My team mates after winning a cup final or League Championship a great feeling of achievement.

Question 9.
What is the most outrageous thing you have ever bought?
A fancy dress outfit.

Question 10.
Would you agree with England's Ian Wright that the feeling of scoring a goal is better than sex?
Various people have different thoughts and actions.

Robert Molenaar

LEEDS UNITED FOOTBALL CLUB

Question 1.
Which football manager do you respect the most and why?
Hans Van Derzee, Sparta Rotterdam.
Because he listens to his players.

Question 2.
How do you feel about the introduction of video evidence and reversible decisions during and after the match?
Good idea, in theory.

Question 3.
What has been your most memorable professional moment and your most embarrassing personal moment?
Debut at Elland Road. Own goal 4-5 years ago, Volendam at PSV!

Question 4.
If you could change any of the rules in football what would it be?
Try to do something about diving.

Question 5.
You're playing in the cup final. It's 0-0 in the 89th minute. You're tackled by a defender in the penalty box. Would you think about taking a dive to get a penalty?
Yes! Of course

Question 6.
Do you have an alternative career plan for the day when you retire from professional football?
I don't know yet.

Question 7.
What has been your funniest experience when travelling with your team?
The sunroof came loose on the way to Liverpool and the physio had to fix it. Physio David Swift and Kit man Sean Hardy stood up holding it on all the way to Liverpool.

Question 8.
Who would you most like to have an Amstel Beer with in the hot tub with you after a big match?
Christy Brinkley, Demi Moore, Pamela Anderson to see if they float!

Question 9.
What is the most outrageous thing you have ever bought?
I never bought anything outrageous. I am too sensible.

Question 10.
Would you agree with England's Ian Wright that the feeling of scoring a goal is better than sex?
No.

Brian Mooney

BOHEMIAN FOOTBALL CLUB

Question 1.
Which football manager do you respect the most and why?
John McGrath (Preston) - good man management

Question 2.
How do you feel about the introduction of video evidence and reversible decisions during and after the match?
Good Idea.

Question 3.
What has been your most memorable professional moment and your most embarrassing personal moment?
4 - 1 Ireland V England. B International.

Question 4.
If you could change any of the rules in football what would it be?
Penalty shoot out.

Question 5.
You're playing in the cup final. It's 0 - 0 in the 89th minute. You're tackled by a defender in the penalty box. Would you think about taking a dive to get a penalty?
Yes.

Question 6.
Do you have an alternative career plan for the day when you retire from professional football?
Yes.

Question 7.
What has been your funniest experience when travelling with your team?
No comment.

Question 8.
Who would you most like to have an Amstel Beer with in the hot tub with you after a big match?
Girlfriend.

Question 9.
What is the most outrageous thing you have ever bought?
Engagement Ring.

Question 10.
Would you agree with England's Ian Wright that the feeling of scoring a goal is better than sex?
No

Alan Moore

MIDDLESBROUGH FOOTBALL CLUB

Question 1.
Which football manager do you respect the most and why?
Mick McCarthy, because I want to play for Ireland.

Question 2.
How do you feel about the introduction of video evidence and reversible decisions during and after the match?
I think that would take an important part of football away just look at Jeff Hurst's goal in the World Cup Final. People still talk about that goal in pubs nowadays. All that would change so its not a good thing.

Question 3.
What has been your most memorable professional moment and your most embarrassing personal moment?
Making my debut for Ireland was the best ever and most embarrassing coming on as a sub after 20 minutes and not getting a touch.

Question 4.
If you could change any of the rules in football what would it be?
Shorten matches, about 10 minutes each way!

Question 5.
You're playing in the cup final. It's 0-0 in the 89th minute. You're tackled by a defender in the penalty box. Would you think about taking a dive to get a penalty?
Yes! Think of the win bonus.

Question 6.
Do you have an alternative career plan for the day when you retire from professional football?
No, not at the moment, but the golf is coming on well!

Question 7.
What has been your funniest experience when travelling with your team?
On one break to Spain a certain player lost his eyebrows and had a role shaved in the back of his head with "666" wrote on it after a drinking session.

Question 8.
Who would you most like to have an Amstel Beer with in the hot tub with you after a big match?
Liz Hurley.

Question 9.
What is the most outrageous thing you have ever bought?
No comment

Question 10.
Would you agree with England's Ian Wright that the feeling of scoring a goal is better than sex?
No, not really if you score a goal ten blokes kiss you. Whereas with sex it's a girlie who's kissing you isn't it.

Eoin Mullen

BOHEMIAN FOOTBALL CLUB

Question 1.
Which football manager do you respect the most and why?
The one that will give me my next contract.

Question 2.
How do you feel about the introduction of video evidence and reversible decisions during and after the match?
Video's yes, for off the ball incidents. No, for penalties etc. during the game.

Question 3.
What has been your most memorable professional moment and your most embarrassing personal moment?
Most memorable moment was winning the league in 93/94.

Question 4.
If you could change any of the rules in football what would it be?
Always two left footers in every team.

Question 5.
You're playing in the cup final. It's 0 - 0 in the 89th minute. You're tackled by a defender in the penalty box. Would you think about taking a dive to get a penalty?
89th minute!! No way I'd be in the box!!

Question 6.
Do you have an alternative career plan for the day when you retire from professional football?
No

Question 7.
What has been your funniest experience when travelling with your team?
Leaving 4 lads at a Budapest hotel (and I was one of them!)

Question 8.
Who would you most like to have an Amstel Beer with in the hot tub with you after a big match?
The female Baywatch cast!

Question 9.
What is the most outrageous thing you have ever bought?
Engagement ring!

Question 10.
Would you agree with England's Ian Wright that the feeling of scoring a goal is better than sex?
Depends on the goal, did it deflect in off your shin, or did you beat 3 men and score from 30 yards.

Mick Neville

SHELBOURNE FOOTBALL CLUB

Question 1.
Which football manager do you respect the most and why?
Jim McLoughlin (Dundalk). Because there was more to him than just football. He takes a great interest in his players and always seemed to know when players were distracted from their football. Be it work, family problems or whatever. Very few managers tune in to that side. From a football sense he is simply the best. Doesn't say a lot but misses nothing. Treats the players as ADULTS.

Question 2.
How do you feel about the introduction of video evidence and reversible decisions during and after the match?
As a defender I think it's good and bad. Good because I think honesty would prevail as a lot of forwards tend to take advantage of new rules which suit them (Diving). Bad because I might miss a tackle and get away with it from a kind referee, but I'd be caught on cameras (not for the first time).

MICK NEVILLE - SHELBOURNE FOOTBALL CLUB

Question 3.
What has been your most memorable professional moment and your most embarrassing personal moment?
Playing anytime for the League of Ireland - Representing Ireland Olympic Qualifiers. But captaining Shelbourne to both the League title and then the FAI Cup at times when we were under-dogs was a great thrill -v- St. Pats Cup Final. The 6 - 4 defeat by Shamrock Rovers a couple of seasons ago. I think I was responsible for 4 of their goals (Bad day at the office!).

Question 4.
If you could change any of the rules in football what would it be?
I think forwards get away with murder I think the referees nearly always go the way of the attacker. Possibly to make the game more exciting. Sorry the rule change I would make would be to kick lumps off the centre forward without being penalised for once it's very difficult for defenders these days.

Question 5.
You're playing in the cup final. It's 0 -0 all in the 89th minute. You're tackled by a defender in the penalty box. Would you think about taking a dive to get a penalty?
Absolutely.

Question 6.
Do you have an alternative career plan for the day when you retire from professional football?
I do, everybody tells me I'm going to be a manager. But I will take things step by step at the moment. I am Youth Development Officer with Shelbourne FC. I hold an International Coaching Badge and hope to do my full Coaching Badge in the near future. I manage the U19's Shelbourne Youth Team and over-see Shelbourne Schoolboys with my assistant Ken McCarthy. As for the future who knows! Time will tell.

Question 7.
What has been your funniest experience when travelling with your team?
Various away trips with Shelbourne. Derry, Sligo and Waterford. The bus broke down on many occasion's but I think Sligo took the award. We headed back from Sligo 10:00 at night. The first coach broke down and we waited about an hour for a replacement. This arrived and about an hour and a half later ran out of diesel. The gauge was broke and the driver thought the bus had been filled. At the time I nearly cried. We arrived in Dublin at 5am all you could do was laugh (the next day!).

Question 8.
Who would you most like to have an Amstel Beer with in the hot tub with you after a big match?
Sharon Stone, Cindy Crawford, Kim Basinger, The Corrs (Girls), Mariah Carey. It would be quite a big bath, with Amstel on Tap (Hot & Cold!).

Question 9.
What is the most outrageous thing you have ever bought?
God knows, LA LA (Tele Tubbies) for my little girl (Lois).

Question 10.
Would you agree with England's Ian Wright that the feeling of scoring a goal is better than sex?
No way, I have scored once in about 4 years. If that is compared to my sex life I've just lost my virginity at 37.

Tony O'Connor

BOHEMIAN FOOTBALL CLUB

Question 1.
Which football manager do you respect the most and why?
Brian Kerr, he did well for me.

Question 2.
How do you feel about the introduction of video evidence and reversible decisions during and after the match?
Not too much, if it's not broken don't fix it.

Question 3.
What has been your most memorable professional moment and your most embarrassing personal moment?
Most memorable moment was winning the league title.

Question 4.
If you could change any of the rules in football what would it be?
None, there's enough bad rules already.

Question 5.
You're playing in the cup final. It's 0 - 0 in the 89th minute. You're tackled by a defender in the penalty box. Would you think about taking a dive to get a penalty?
I'd think about it and then I'd dive!

Question 6.
Do you have an alternative career plan for the day when you retire from professional football?
None whatsoever.

Question 7.
What has been your funniest experience when travelling with your team?
Being left in Sligo with Maurice O'Driscoll and trying to explain to my wife!

Question 8.
Who would you most like to have an Amstel Beer with in the hot tub with you after a big match?
The girl out of the film "Species"!

Question 9.
What is the most outrageous thing you have ever bought?
DIY equipment!

Question 10.
Would you agree with England's Ian Wright that the feeling of scoring a goal is better than sex?
It depends on who the sex is with and who the team is!

Maurice O'Driscoll

BOHEMIAN FOOTBALL CLUB

Question 1.
Which football manager do you respect the most and why?
Brian Kerr. He gave me my start in League of Ireland.

Question 2.
How do you feel about the introduction of video evidence and reversible decisions during and after the match?
Yes, for off the ball incidents.

Question 3.
What has been your most memorable professional moment and your most embarrassing personal moment?
Winning the League with St. Pats and scoring on that day. Too many to mention.

Question 4.
If you could change any of the rules in football what would it be?
No age limit.

Question 5.
You're playing in the cup final. It's 0-0 in the 89th minute. You're tackled by a defender in the penalty box. Would you think about taking a dive to get a penalty?
Yes!

Question 6.
Do you have an alternative career plan for the day when you retire from professional football?
Spend more time with my family.

Question 7.
What has been your funniest experience when travelling with your team?
Waking up with Tony O'Connor. Away to Sligo the team had left without us. If you could hear Tony and me ringing our wife's to explain!

Question 8.
Who would you most like to have an Amstel Beer with in the hot tub with you after a big match?
The Corrs, without the brother! Or else Lynn! My wife really.

Question 9.
What is the most outrageous thing you have ever bought?
My wedding ring! It cost £30 (crazy money).

Question 10.
Would you agree with England's Ian Wright that the feeling of scoring a goal is better than sex?
No way! Diving off the wardrobe is much better!

Keith O'Neill

REPUBLIC OF IRELAND

Question 1.
Which football manager do you respect the most and why?
Mick McCarthy, he gave me my chance and has always kept faith in my ability.

Question 2.
How do you feel about the introduction of video evidence and reversible decisions during and after the match?
With the amount of money involved in football now, I think it would be a good thing because bad decisions can cost millions.

Question 3.
What has been your most memorable professional moment and your most embarrassing personal moment?
Scoring against Croatia, my first for Ireland. Walking backwards and falling into the stand at Southampton while taking a thrown in!

Question 4.
If you could change any of the rules in football what would it be?
None, it's a great game that doesn't need changing.

Question 5.
You're playing in the cup final. It's 0 -0 all in the 89th minute. You're tackled by a defender in the penalty box. Would you think about taking a dive to get a penalty?
No! I'm an honest lad.

Question 6.
Do you have an alternative career plan for the day when you retire from professional football?
Television.

Question 7.
What has been your funniest experience when travelling with your team?
A player was locked in the toilet on the team coach for 2 hours, it was quite funny listening to him as the door was closed just enough that he could not get out.

Question 8.
Who would you most like to have an Amstel Beer with in the hot tub with you after a big match?
Caprice.

Question 9.
What is the most outrageous thing you have ever bought?
£10,000 watch!

Question 10.
Would you agree with England's Ian Wright that the feeling of scoring a goal is better than sex?
Don't know, never shagged his missus!

Niall Quinn

SUNDERLAND FOOTBALL CLUB

Question 1.
Which football manager do you respect the most and why?
Peter Reid - He's honest (tells you what he thinks whether good or bad). He's fair (if you produce the goods for him he'll reward you). He's loyal (even after many injuries he sticks by those who he feels can do it for him, and he's been very successful on a small budget.

Question 2.
How do you feel about the introduction of video evidence and reversible decisions during and after the match?
It is terrible for referees although it does highlight serious discrepancies with the present system. Hopefully it will lead to a better game although finding a way of doing this and not stopping the game every ten seconds will be hard.

Question 3.
What has been your most memorable professional moment and your most embarrassing personal moment?
My favourite moment was scoring against England at Wembley. My most embarrassing moment was on Question of Sport when I thought John Aldridge was a boxer!

Question 4.
If you could change any of the rules in football what would it be?
I would condense the game into 70 minutes with the clock stopping every time the ball goes out of play. It would mean no time wasting or disputed injury time.

Question 5.
You're playing in the cup final. It's 0 - 0 in the 89th minute. You're tackled by a defender in the penalty box. Would you think about taking a dive to get a penalty?
Unfortunately you never know until you're in that position. I would like to think I wouldn't but who knows, in a flash instant I just might. I'd be very regretful afterwards though.

Question 6.
Do you have an alternative career plan for the day when you retire from professional football?
No, I reckon I'm not cut out for management so I'll just have to wait and see. Perhaps something in the media, although ideally I'd love to do something outdoors.

Question 7.
What has been your funniest experience when travelling with your team?
The flight home from Italia '90 was unbelievable. Anybody who fell asleep had their ties cut off. Picture the scene - $^1/_2$ million fans watch Jack's Army meeting Charles Haughey - about three people have full ties, everyone else had a stump 4 inches long hanging down their shirts!

Question 8.
Who would you most like to have an Amstel Beer with in the hot tub with you after a big match?
Anybody except Jo Brand. She frightens the life out of me.

Question 9.
What is the most outrageous thing you have ever bought?
I bought an 18th century pulpit from an old antique shop. It originated from a church in Derybshire, it cost £1,000 and Gillian wouldn't let me bring it into the house!

Question 10.
Would you agree with England's Ian Wright that the feeling of scoring a goal is better than sex?
Far be it for me to suggest Ian Wright is doing "it" wrong, but I have to disagree. Anyway I've scored hat-tricks on the field but could never manage "3" in 90 minutes after bedtime!!

Damien Richardson

EX MANAGER SHELBOURNE FOOTBALL CLUB

Question 1.
Which football manager do you respect the most and why?
Arsene Wenger, because he's come into a different culture and successfully adapted, and he's married the continental and British styles to great effect in a very short period of time.

Question 2.
How do you feel about the introduction of video evidence and reversible decisions during and after the match?
I don't agree with the use of video during games. Mistakes are a great part of the attraction of sport, but I do think to catch discipline and injustice from that point of view it would be useful.

Question 3.
What has been your most memorable professional moment and your most embarrassing personal moment?
When I was asked to sign for Shamrock Rovers as an 18 year old, and my hero Liam Tuohy came round to ask me, which caused a great commotion in the street. It is still my most abiding moment from being involved in the game. When I once took a corner at Gillingham, who played in a very intimate ground with the crowd very close to you. I wanted to take a quick corner and in trying to look to see when I would kick it, I missed the ball and kicked the

corner flag, which jumped out of the ground and travelled about 5 yards. The Gillingham crowd never let me forget it.

Question 4.
If you could change any of the rules in football what would it be?

I would make the goals six inches higher and wider. We don't want to get like the Americans, but the game is about goals and it would help increase the number of goals, although not in a huge way and therefore it would be a positive move.

Question 5.
You're playing in the cup final. It's 0 -0 all in the 89th minute. You're tackled by a defender in the penalty box. Would you think about taking a dive to get a penalty?

I have to admit I was good at taking dives. I saw it as a reverse justice since as an attacker, I like all strikers, was often a victim of bad tackling so I saw it as evening the score

Question 6.
Do you have an alternative career plan for the day when you retire from professional football?

I always wanted to go to sea. Right through my schooling everything was geared towards that and I even did 2 years training to become a radio officer and but for Liam Tuohy who asked me to play football I probably would have gone to sea.

Question 7.
What has been your funniest experience when travelling with your team?

When I was manager of Cork City travelling with the team to go to Istanbul. We were in Heathrow waiting for a flight out, and I told one of the younger players Fergus O'Donohue to hurry up the flight was ready. I stood by the escalator that was coming up and told Fergus to quickly go down it. He ran onto the escalator he thought was going down. All the other players witnessed him falling all over the place and soon everyone was in hysterics.

Question 8.
Who would you most like to have an Amstel Beer with in the hot tub with you after a big match?
Beethoven, because I'd love to know what he was about and to know how that big lump of hair would react to a hot tub.

Question 9.
What is the most outrageous thing you have ever bought?
I bought a pair of flair's in the 60's on the Kings Road during the hay day. They were bright yellow with a flower motif and the reaction to them in Dublin is but described as horrific.

Question 10.
Would you agree with England's Ian Wright that the feeling of scoring a goal is better than sex?
Yes, I don't think words can describe the release you get from scoring a goal, particularly an important one. To me it's one of the greatest feelings to score an important goal in a big match at a vital time. The reaction of yourself, your team mates and the crowd is something I'd like everyone to be able to experience. It's incomparable.

Bobby Robson

MANAGER PSV FOOTBALL CLUB

Question 1.
Which football manager do you respect the most and why?
My mentor. Sir Walter Winterbottom. England team manager for me in World Cup 1958 & 1962.

Question 2.
How do you feel about the introduction of video evidence and reversible decisions during and after the match?
I would only accept video evidence on footballs crossing the lines for legitimate goals, nothing else.

Question 3.
What has been your most memorable professional moment and your most embarrassing personal moment?
Appointed England manager in 1982. Embarrassing moment: Too many I guess to nominate one!

Question 4.
If you could change any of the rules in football what would it be?
Players retreating another ten yards further back when disputing a referees decision for a free kick.

Question 5.
You're playing in the cup final. It's 0-0 in the 89th minute. You're tackled by a defender in the penalty box. Would you think about taking a dive to get a penalty?
I think so, but I would make it look good. In reality, No.

Question 6.
Do you have an alternative career plan for the day when you retire from professional football?
Yes. Holidays, more golf and see more of my family. i.e. three sons & four grandchildren. A wonderful alternative plan to working.

Question 7.
What has been your funniest experience when travelling with your team?
Having Paul Gasgoigne around me for 7 weeks in Italia '90 World Cup!

Question 8.
Who would you most like to have an Amstel Beer with in the hot tub with you after a big match?
The World Cup winning English Team of 1966, yes all of them!

Question 9.
What is the most outrageous thing you have ever bought?
I try not to buy outrageous things! I bought "Ronaldo" for 20 million dollars (US). But that wasn't outrageous.

Question 10.
Would you agree with England's Ian Wright that the feeling of scoring a goal is better than sex?
What a Question! Only Ian Wright can answer that!

Bryan Robson

MANAGER MIDDLESBROUGH FOOTBALL CLUB

Question 1.
Which football manager do you respect the most and why?
Alex Ferguson. Unbelievable record with Manchester United.

Question 2.
How do you feel about the introduction of video evidence and reversible decisions during and after the match?
I think if the offence is so bad and the referee did not see it or did see it wrong then video evidence is good.

Question 3.
What has been your most memorable professional moment and your most embarrassing personal moment?
Winning the European Cup Winners Cup in 1991 with Manchester United.

Question 4.
If you could change any of the rules in football what would it be?
Just petty yellow and red cards. They drive me mad.

Question 5.
You're playing in the cup final. It's 0 - 0 in the 89th minute. You're tackled by a defender in the penalty box. Would you think about taking a dive to get a penalty?
No. I would think about scoring a goal.

Question 6.
Do you have an alternative career plan for the day when you retire from professional football?
Yes, retirement.

Question 7.
What has been your funniest experience when travelling with your team?
We arrived at a supposed hotel in Sweden for pre-season matches, it was a camp site next to a long distance lorry drive filling station (with Middlesbrough).

Question 8.
Who would you most like to have an Amstel Beer with in the hot tub with you after a big match?
Another 23 Amstel Beers!!

Question 9.
What is the most outrageous thing you have ever bought?
A pair of 9" platform shoes for a mate of mine!

Question 10.
Would you agree with England's Ian Wright that the feeling of scoring a goal is better than sex?
Depends!

Simon Rodger

CRYSTAL PALACE FOOTBALL CLUB

Question 1.
Which football manager do you respect the most and why?
Alex Ferguson, because he has won everything in the game and he motivates his players so well.

Question 2.
How do you feel about the introduction of video evidence and reversible decisions during and after the match?
I think it's a great idea because the referee can't always see the right decision.

Question 3.
What has been your most memorable professional moment and your most embarrassing personal moment?
My most memorable professional moment was winning the First Division Championship My most embarrassing moment would be probably missing an easy scoring chance.

Question 4.
If you could change any of the rules in football what would it be?
I would get rid of the offside rule because it would make the game more exciting.

Question 5.
You're playing in the cup final. It's 0 - 0 in the 89th minute. You're tackled by a defender in the penalty box. Would you think about taking a dive to get a penalty?
No I could never take a dive in the penalty box, because I'm too honest and it's cheating

Question 6.
Do you have an alternative career plan for the day when you retire from professional football?
Yes, I'm going into business with my wife and her mum and dad, they own a mortgage company.

Question 7.
What has been your funniest experience when travelling with your team?
When travelling to one certain match, we stopped off for some petrol and we could not get the petrol cap off. So we ended up missing the match, that was a funny experience.

Question 8.
Who would you most like to have an Amstel Beer with in the hot tub with you after a big match?
The hot tub would not be big enough for all the women I'd like to have in there with me.

Question 9.
What is the most outrageous thing you have ever bought?
A blow - up doll!

Question 10.
Would you agree with England's Ian Wright that the feeling of scoring a goal is better than sex?
Ian Wright must be doing it wrong!

Lee Sharpe

LEEDS UNITED FOOTBALL CLUB

Question 1.
Which football manager do you respect the most and why?
Cyril Knowles (late). He gave me my first chance in football.

Question 2.
How do you feel about the introduction of video evidence and reversible decisions during and after the match?
In certain situations - it stops the flow of the game.

Question 3.
What has been your most memorable professional moment and your most embarrassing personal moment?
Winning the Cup Winners Cup with Manchester United. Nothing springs to mind, as it takes a lot to embarrass me.

Question 4.
If you could change any of the rules in football what would it be?
No one would be allowed to tackle in the attacking third of the pitch.

Question 5.
You're playing in the cup final. It's 0 -0 all in the 89th minute. You're tackled by a defender in the penalty box. Would you think about taking a dive to get a penalty?
It depends where I am in the box, if I can get a clear shot, or not.

Question 6.
Do you have an alternative career plan for the day when you retire from professional football?
Yes, professional golfer and entrepreneur and a dirty rotten scoundrel!

Question 7.
What has been your funniest experience when travelling with your team?
On the way back from a match all the lads were banging on the back window at two girls in a car and one girl stood up and flashed her boobs through the sunroof!

Question 8.
Who would you most like to have an Amstel Beer with in the hot tub with you after a big match?
Kylie and Danni Minogue, Demi Moore, Gwyneth Paltrow, Mariah Carey, a couple of the Corrs and my mate Christy.

Question 9.
What is the most outrageous thing you have ever bought?
17 years old I bought a Renault 5 GT Turbo. I thought I was so cool.

Question 10.
Would you agree with England's Ian Wright that the feeling of scoring a goal is better than sex?
No. He is obviously doing it wrong.

Tim Sherwood

BLACKBURN ROVERS FOOTBALL CLUB.

Question 1.
Which football manager do you respect the most and why?
Kenny Dalglish - Manager of
Blackburn when we won the league.

Question 2.
How do you feel about the introduction of video evidence and reversible decisions during and after the match?
Leave the game as it is.

Question 3.
What has been your most memorable professional moment and your most embarrassing personal moment?
Lifting Premiership trophy - most memorable. No embarrassing moments.

Question 4.
If you could change any of the rules in football what would it be?
No - wouldn't change anything!

Question 5.
You're playing in the cup final. It's 0 - 0 in the 89th minute. You're tackled by a defender in the penalty box. Would you think about taking a dive to get a penalty?
Yes

Question 6.
Do you have an alternative career plan for the day when you retire from professional football?
I won't need to work, I'll keep busy with my hobbies.

Question 7.
What has been your funniest experience when travelling with your team?
Back window of bus exploded on M6 due to heat from ovens.

Question 8.
Who would you most like to have an Amstel Beer with in the hot tub with you after a big match?
The man of the Match.

Question 9.
What is the most outrageous thing you have ever bought?
Pair of football boots!

Question 10.
Would you agree with England's Ian Wright that the feeling of scoring a goal is better than sex?
No.

Jim Smith

MANAGER DERBY COUNTY FOOTBALL CLUB

Question 1.

Which football manager do you respect the most and why?

Alex Ferguson, he's a winner.

Question 2.

How do you feel about the introduction of video evidence and reversible decisions during and after the match?

Only in goal line decisions during the match Sending off, bookings after the match.

Question 3.

What has been your most memorable professional moment and your most embarrassing personal moment?

Memorable: Managing Derby County to the Premier

Embarassing: The Laws in South Korea (In a phone booth!) Enough Said

Question 4.

If you could change any of the rules in football what would it be?

Offside

Question 5.
You're playing in the cup final. It's 0 - 0 in the 89th minute. You're tackled by a defender in the penalty box. Would you think about taking a dive to get a penalty?
Yes.

Question 6.
Do you have an alternative career plan for the day when you retire from professional football?
Enjoy myself.

Question 7.
What has been your funniest experience when travelling with your team?
Being left behind at Doncaster when managing Oxford.

Question 8.
Who would you most like to have an Amstel Beer with in the hot tub with you after a big match?
No comment.

Question 9.
What is the most outrageous thing you have ever bought?
Tailor made suit in South Korea UGH!!

Question 10.
Would you agree with England's Ian Wright that the feeling of scoring a goal is better than sex?
Never scored an important enough goal.

Alex Stepney

EX MANCHESTER UNITED

Question 1.
Which football manager do you respect the most and why?
Sir Matt Busby because he gave myself and my family the utmost respect. He even took us looking for houses around Manchester when I first arrived after my transfer from Chelsea.

Question 2.
How do you feel about the introduction of video evidence and reversible decisions during and after the match?
I think that eventually this will be used only in the penalty area, for penalty decision's and if the ball crossed the goal line.

Question 3.
What has been your most memorable professional moment and your most embarrassing personal moment?
Playing for my country. Pat Jennings scoring against me in the Charity Shield 1967. (But I also scored two goals in my career!)

Question 4.
If you could change any of the rules in football what would it be?
I would make referees professional. Making them train with their local teams to understand certain situations.

Question 5.
You're playing in the cup final. It's 0 - 0 in the 89th minute. You're tackled by a defender in the penalty box. Would you think about taking a dive to get a penalty?
Not applicable. If I was an outfield player, Yes!

Question 6.
Did you have an alternative career plan for the day when you retired from professional football?
At the age of 56 I now am goalkeeping coach with Manchester United.

Question 7.
What has been your funniest experience when travelling with your team?
Seeing the club's Don Juan pulling a transvestite without knowing, on a flight from L.A. to Toronto.

Question 8.
Who would you most like to have an Amstel Beer with in the hot tub with you after a big match?
My wife. Then she would realise the need to relax after a game.

Question 9.
What is the most outrageous thing you have ever bought?
Dallas style suit with boots and Stetson and wearing them in England!

Question 10.
Would you agree with England's Ian Wright that the feeling of scoring a goal is better than sex?
No, A goal only takes 1 second!

Steve Staunton

REPUBLIC OF IRELAND

Question 1.
Which football manager do you respect the most and why?
Kenny Dalglish, because of what he achieved in the game as a player.

Question 2.
How do you feel about the introduction of video evidence and reversible decisions during and after the match?
Not during a match, but maybe used to over turn wrongful yellow or red cards.

Question 3.
What has been your most memorable professional moment and your most embarrassing personal moment?
Playing for Ireland -v- Italy in the quarter finals of World Cup in 1990.

Question 4.
If you could change any of the rules in football what would it be?
I'd have no offside in the penalty box.

Question 5.
You're playing in the cup final. It's 0 - 0 in the 89th minute. You're tackled by a defender in the penalty box. Would you

think about taking a dive to get a penalty?
No, I wouldn't dive.

Question 6.
Do you have an alternative career plan for the day when you retire from professional football?
No, not at this moment in time.

Question 7.
What has been your funniest experience when travelling with your team?
On pre-season tour and seeing Ronnie Whelan come down to dinner dressed all in white.

Question 8.
Who would you most like to have an Amstel Beer with in the hot tub with you after a big match?
I suppose I should say my wife, but I think it would have to be Jennifer Aniston.

Question 9.
What is the most outrageous thing you have ever bought?
No comment.

Question 10.
Would you agree with England's Ian Wright that the feeling of scoring a goal is better than sex?
No, because I hardly score!

Nobby Stiles

EX MANCHESTER UNITED & ENGLAND

Question 1.
Which football manager do you respect the most and why?
Sir Mat Busby, he was a joy to work for. Sir Alf Ramsey, great to play under Alex Ferguson, the job he has done with Man. U, he is so far ahead of his time.

Question 2.
How do you feel about the introduction of video evidence and reversible decisions during and after the match?
Well, I think it is because of the camera's, there are so many camera's these days. In my time there was no camera's. The referees if they made a mistake we always said over the season it would even up. They have to make split decisions.

Question 3.
What has been your most memorable professional moment and your most embarrassing personal moment?
66 World cup final, I am so proud of it. Playing for England at 1st International against Scotland at Wembley, we went into Cafe Royal for a big function afterwards in the evening. I went out to the toilets and came back in about an hour and half after sat down at the table and they asked me where I'd been. I went into the wrong function room, sat at the table talking away and I realised I was at a Jewish Wedding.

Question 4.
If you could change any of the rules in football what would it be?
Wouldn't change any of the rules. No passing back has opened up

the game. It's a great rule.

Question 5.
You're playing in the cup final. It's 0 -0 all in the 89th minute. You're tackled by a defender in the penalty box. Would you think about taking a dive to get a penalty?
No doubt about it, you'd have to! It's a natural reaction, not really cheating.

Question 6.
Did you have an alternative career plan for the day when you retired from professional football?
I thought I had, lot's of people will give you advice as to what to do when you retire. My advice to kid's today is to look at it in 10/15 years times, they're earning great money just look after it.

Question 7.
What has been your funniest experience when travelling with your team?
Bobby Charlton, Shay Ben and I were good mates and we used to play a game called cribbage, we played for orders! Not for money. England World Cup we'd get off the coach, three bags, three cases under my arm I would be carrying them in and Shay would say "Happy" and he'd have a fag in his mouth and I'd have to light it!

Question 8.
Who would you most like to have an Amstel Beer with in the hot tub with you after a big match?
Duncan Evans, greatest player I ever saw.

Question 9.
What is the most outrageous thing you have ever bought?
Never been outrageous really, I'm a boring bastard really.

Question 10.
Would you agree with England's Ian Wright that the feeling of scoring a goal is better than sex?
I never scored so I wouldn't know the feeling.

Andy Townsend

MIDDLESBROUGH FOOTBALL CLUB

Question 1.
Which football manager do you respect the most and why?
Big Jack. Good laugh, loyal and honest and players will always respond to that.

Question 2.
How do you feel about the introduction of video evidence and reversible decisions during and after the match?
It won't affect me because I'm retiring soon.

Question 3.
What has been your most memorable professional moment and your most embarrassing personal moment?
Jack Charlton farted in front of Albert Reynolds and then blamed me! My most memorable moment was leading the team out in New York against Italy in 1994 World Cup.

Question 4.
If you could change any of the rules in football what would it be?
I'd change the game from 45 minutes each way to about 5 minutes each way!

Question 5.
You're playing in the cup final. It's 0 - 0 in the 89th minute. You're tackled by a defender in the penalty box. Would you think about taking a dive to get a penalty?
Yes! Absolutely, definitely, no question (I think!).

Question 6.
Do you have an alternative career plan for the day when you retire from professional football?
Yes. I'm going into boxing. "Sugar Puff Townsend!"

Question 7.
What has been your funniest experience when travelling with your team?
After training with the Irish Team we used to sing to Big Jack on the coach and he would pull over to the nearest pub and buy us a few pints. Before the quarter final of the 1990 World Cup Jack had a "Guinness Bar" brought to the hotel and we got half pissed before the game!

Question 8.
Who would you most like to have an Amstel Beer with in the hot tub with you after a big match?
How big is the bath? Can I have more than one? I think it would have to be Carmen Electra or Liz Hurley or Jenny McCarthey.

Question 9.
What is the most outrageous thing you have ever bought?
Harley Davison. We're not allowed to ride them and I had not passed my test!

Question 10.
Would you agree with England's Ian Wright that the feeling of scoring a goal is better than sex?
No. I can't remember because I haven't scored a goal for a while.

Cyril Walsh

ST. PATRICK'S FOOTBALL CLUB

Question 1.
Which football manager do you respect the most and why?
Brian Kerr. Achievements & ability. Can make a good team out of Sparse resources.

Question 2.
How do you feel about the introduction of video evidence and reversible decisions during and after the match?
During - not a good idea. After - very positive developments especially regarding appeals.

Question 3.
What has been your most memorable professional moment and your most embarrassing personal moment?
Most memorable. Winning the League, Dundalk '96. Most embarrassing. Can't think of any!

Question 4.
If you could change any of the rules in football what would it be?
Rules are OK. Implementation and abuse is the problem.Consistency of interpretation is needed.

Question 5.
You're playing in the cup final. It's 0-0 in the 89th minute. You're tackled by a defender in the penalty box. Would you think about taking a dive to get a penalty?
Yes.

Question 6.
Do you have an alternative career plan for the day when you retire from professional football?
No.

Question 7.
What has been your funniest experience when travelling with your team?
Opposing player travelling on bus! Stopped for a few minutes, forgot we had another passenger, and left him in Clonmel!

Question 8.
Who would you most like to have an Amstel Beer with in the hot tub with you after a big match?
My partner.

Question 9.
What is the most outrageous thing you have ever bought?
Donald Duck boxer shorts.

Question 10.
Would you agree with England's Ian Wright that the feeling of scoring a goal is better than sex?
He's not doing it right or else he's having sex with the wrong person.

David Wetherall

LEEDS UNITED FOOTBALL CLUB

Question 1.
Which football manager do you respect the most and why?
Wilko. Because he gave me my first break and took Leeds to League Champions from nowhere.

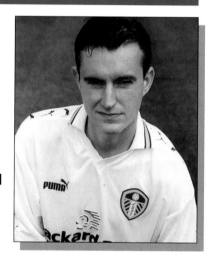

Question 2.
How do you feel about the introduction of video evidence and reversible decisions during and after the match?
It can only go so far - it interrupt's the flow of the game.

Question 3.
What has been your most memorable professional moment and your most embarrassing personal moment?
Running out at Wembley in the Coca Cola Cup 1996. Sword fighting with "House For Sale" signs when I was a student and I got a slap on the wrist from the police!

Question 4.
If you could change any of the rules in football what would it be?
Compulsory booking for any player who dives.

Question 5.
You're playing in the cup final. It's 0-0 in the 89th minute. You're tackled by a defender in the penalty box. Would you think about taking a dive to get a penalty?
No I would just score anyway!

Question 6.
Do you have an alternative career plan for the day when you retire from professional football?
Not yet.

Question 7.
What has been your funniest experience when travelling with your team?
See Sharpies!! (page 173)

Question 8.
Who would you most like to have an Amstel Beer with in the hot tub with you after a big match?
Cindy Crawford, Jennifer Aniston, Denise Van Outen, Kylie Minogue.

Question 9.
What is the most outrageous thing you have ever bought?
Nothing, because I am too tight!

Question 10.
Would you agree with England's Ian Wright that the feeling of scoring a goal is better than sex?
No chance, not even close. That is why I am a defender not a centre forward.

Gareth Whalley

REPUBLIC OF IRELAND

Question 1.
Which football manager do you respect the most and why?
Apart from my own, Martin O'Neill for what he has done at Leister and Alex Ferguson for his principles about the way the game should be played.

Question 2.
How do you feel about the introduction of video evidence and reversible decisions during and after the match?
Not a bad idea for during the match as long as you don't hold the play up too long. But not for after the match as it's too late to change things.

Question 3.
What has been your most memorable professional moment and your most embarrassing personal moment?
Promotion with my club team, plus selection for the Irish Squad .

Question 4.
If you could change any of the rules in football what would it be?
Probably video evidence to help referees during the game.

Question 5.
You're playing in the cup final. It's 0 - 0 in the 89th minute. You're tackled by a defender in the penalty box. Would you think about taking a dive to get a penalty?
Yes!

Question 6.
Do you have an alternative career plan for the day when you retire from professional football?
No not yet.

Question 7.
What has been your funniest experience when travelling with your team?
No Comment

Question 8.
Who would you most like to have an Amstel Beer with in the hot tub with you after a big match?
Apart from my wife. A young Raquel Welch

Question 9.
What is the most outrageous thing you have ever bought?
No Comment.

Question 10.
Would you agree with England's Ian Wright that the feeling of scoring a goal is better than sex?
No you can not compare them. They're both great in different ways!

Clyde Wijnhard

LEEDS UNITED FOOTBALL CLUB

Question 1.
Which football manager do you respect the most and why?
Louis Valgaal. He made me a good footballer.

Question 2.
How do you feel about the introduction of video evidence and reversible decisions during and after the match?
Crap!

Question 3.
What has been your most memorable professional moment and your most embarrassing personal moment?
When I scored my first goal. And when I was sent off last week!

Question 4.
If you could change any of the rules in football what would it be?
Better referees!

Question 5.
You're playing in the cup final. It's 0-0 in the 89th minute. You're tackled by a defender in the penalty box. Would you think about taking a dive to get a penalty?
Yes. .

Question 6.

Do you have an alternative career plan for the day when you retire from professional football?
Go around the world.

Question 7.

What has been your funniest experience when travelling with your team?
Stuck in the lift at Leeds Bradford Airport.

Question 8.

Who would you most like to have an Amstel Beer with in the hot tub with you after a big match?
Halle Berry.

Question 9.

What is the most outrageous thing you have ever bought?
Lots of clothes.

Question 10.

Would you agree with England's Ian Wright that the feeling of scoring a goal is better than sex?
No.

Darren Williams

SUNDERLAND FOOTBALL CLUB

Question 1.
Which football manager do you respect the most and why?
Jack Charlton, because he had a great career in football and performed some great things with the Rep. of Ireland team. He is very honest in the way he does things.

Question 2.
How do you feel about the introduction of video evidence and reversible decisions during and after the match?
I'm not for it because it will slow the game down and take away the excitement having to stop and watch what happened over again.

Question 3.
What has been your most memorable professional moment and your most embarrassing personal moment?
Playing for York against Man. United and beating them in the Coca Cola Cup.

Question 4.
If you could change any of the rules in football what would it be?
I would change the banned rule for the yellow cards. I think it should be increased on the amount of yellow cards you can pick up before a ban.

Question 5.
You're playing in the cup final. It's 0 - 0 in the 89th minute. You're tackled by a defender in the penalty box. Would you think about taking a dive to get a penalty?
Yes! It meant we get a penalty for my team to be able to win the game.

Question 6.
Do you have an alternative career plan for the day when you retire from professional football?
Yes, I would like to get into football coaching or have my own clothes shop.

Question 7.
What has been your funniest experience when travelling with your team?
We were travelling back after a game and one of the lads (best left unnamed!) fell down the stairs at the back of the bus and hit the back down

Question 8.
Who would you most like to have an Amstel Beer with in the hot tub with you after a big match?
I would like to have Amstel Beer in a hot tub with Sandra Bullock. But please don't tell the girl friend!

Question 9.
What is the most outrageous thing you have ever bought?
I bought a D & G top because it looked nice, but I was just kidding myself, because it wouldn't have fit an Action Man figure!

Question 10.
Would you agree with England's Ian Wright that the feeling of scoring a goal is better than sex?
I don't really know I don't often score goals so I can't compare. But I could ask Kevin Philips, he's scored a few so I guess he has a good sex life!

Paul Williams

COVENTRY CITY FOOTBALL CLUB

Question 1.
Which football manager do you respect the most and why?
Ruud Gullit - Newcastle. Just his way of management.

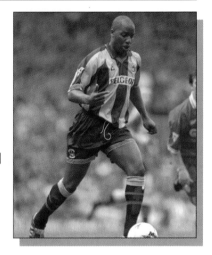

Question 2.
How do you feel about the introduction of video evidence and reversible decisions during and after the match?
It's a good thing to allow or disallow goals.

Question 3.
What has been your most memorable professional moment and your most embarrassing personal moment?
Memorable: Scoring my first hat-trick. Embarrassing: None!

Question 4.
If you could change any of the rules in football what would it be?
None.

Question 5.
You're playing in the cup final. It's 0 - 0 in the 89th minute. You're tackled by a defender in the penalty box. Would you think about taking a dive to get a penalty?
Yes! Because it is all about winning.

Question 6.
Do you have an alternative career plan for the day when you retire from professional football?
Yes, I want to go into business in some capacity.

Question 7.
What has been your funniest experience when travelling with your team?
When Darren Huckerby asked to put a funny video on when we had just got beaten.

Question 8.
Who would you most like to have an Amstel Beer with in the hot tub with you after a big match?
Lynn our secretary at the Training Ground.

Question 9.
What is the most outrageous thing you have ever bought?
A jacket and our manager at the time Arthur Cox, gave me so much stick he said I looked like Luther Vandross!

Question 10.
Would you agree with England's Ian Wright that the feeling of scoring a goal is better than sex?
No.

Danny Wilson

MANAGER SHEFFIELD WEDNESDAY FOOTBALL CLUB

Question 1.

Which football manager do you respect the most and why?

In English football it would have to be Alex Ferguson. The way he has had Manchester United dominate the domestic scene over the last few years has been excellent. The "home grown" talent he has nurtured has to be respected. Abroad it would for me be "Bobby Robson" who has gone to numerous countries and been very successful, when everybody is saying foreign coaches are the best in the world, we arguably have the best 2.

Question 2.

How do you feel about the introduction of video evidence and reversible decisions during and after the match?

What you have to consider is whether or not the decision to call on video evidence during the game will stop the flow of football and pace of the game. We cannot afford to be having games stopped every few minutes because the referee wants his decisions to be perfect. For penalty decisions I would agree, but not any others nor reversing the decision after the game.

Question 3.

What has been your most memorable professional moment and your most embarrassing personal moment?

I think signing my first professional contract, playing at international level with Northern Ireland, playing at Wembley on numerous Cup Finals and getting promotion as manager at Barnsley against all the odds. My most embarrassing moment was "following through" whilst playing for Bury and having to rush off the field to "finish off" and get changed.

Question 4.

If you could change any of the rules in football what would it be?

Stop these stupid "stretcher - bearers" coming onto the field to so called "speed the game up". What a load of "Codswallop" that is.

Question 5.

You're playing in the cup final. It's 0 - 0 in the 89th minute. You're tackled by a defender in the penalty box. Would you think about taking a dive to get a penalty?

No. I have never as a player done that type of thing and I would never either encourage or condone that type of tactic no matter what the prize was.

Question 6.

Do you have an alternative career plan for the day when you retire from professional football?

Football has always been my life, so really I would hope it could continue for the foreseeable future. But precarious as the job is, I could always turn my hand to digging a hole if need be, that type of thing has never scared me.

Question 7.
What has been your funniest experience when travelling with your team?
Only leaving a couple players and a Director in a motorway service station, thinking they were on the coach.

Question 8.
Who would you most like to have an Amstel Beer with in the hot tub with you after a big match?
It would have to be Olivia Newton John. For some unknown reason, I have had a crush on her since I was about 10 years old!

Question 9.
What is the most outrageous thing you have ever bought?
Nothing really outrageous apart from the Sex Pistols album in its heyday.

Question 10.
Would you agree with England's Ian Wright that the feeling of scoring a goal is better than sex?
Certainly not. My local massage parlour would never forgive me if I did. They could all be out on the local football pitch, trying to score!